The Attitudes of Ethnic Minorities

by Simon Field

**A HOME OFFICE
RESEARCH AND PLANNING UNIT
REPORT**

LONDON: HER MAJESTY'S STATIONERY OFFICE

ISBN 0 11 340774 2

305.8
FIE

HOME OFFICE RESEARCH STUDIES

'Home Office Research Studies' comprise reports on research undertaken in the Home Office to assist in the exercise of its administrative functions, and for the information of the judicature, the services for which the Home Secretary has responsibility (direct or indirect) and the general public.

On the last pages of this report are listed titles already published in this series, in the preceding series *Studies in the Causes of Delinquency and the Treatment of Offenders,* and in the series of *Research and Planning Unit Papers.*

267400

Her Majesty's Stationery Office

Standing order service

Placing a standing order with HMSO BOOKS enables a customer to receive other titles in this series automatically as published.

This saves the time, trouble and expense of placing individual orders and avoids the problem of knowing when to do so.

For details please write to HMSO BOOKS (PC 13A/1), Publications Centre, PO Box 276, London SW8 5DT and quoting reference X25.08.07.

The standing order service also enables customers to receive automatically as published all material of their choice which additionally saves extensive catalogue research. The scope and selectivity of the service has been extended by new techniques, and there are more than 3,500 classifications to choose from. A special leaflet describing the service in detail may be obtained on request.

Foreword

Many claims have been made about the attitudes of ethnic minorities towards themselves, towards whites and towards British institutions, which, if true, would have serious implications for race relations. These claims have included the view that ethnic minorities lack self respect because of their disadvantaged position, that young blacks are 'alienated', and that young blacks and Asians have unrealistic job aspirations. This review of the research literature examines the evidence bearing on these among other propositions.

Much of the evidence is negative: in many respects the attitudes of blacks and Asians living in Britain do not differ dramatically from those of whites. While there are exceptions to this rule, and further research is needed in some fields, these findings suggest that more caution is needed in future about accepting judgments made about black and Asian attitudes.

R. V. G. CLARKE
Head of the Research and Planning Unit

Contents

1 Introduction

The aim of this paper is to review the research literature on the attitudes of blacks and Asians living in Britain, and to discuss the implications of the research findings. In this paper, the term 'ethnic minorities' may be taken to refer to these blacks and Asians, the vast majority of whom are of New Commonwealth or Pakistani ethnic origin. The primary concern of the paper will be those attitudes which directly bear on race relations, which often arise from the experience of immigration or from ethnic minority status as such, rather than from more specific cultural roots. It follows that this survey will deal only tangentially with the subtler features of ethnic minority cultures, since many of these features are only indirectly relevant to relations between the races and to policies applicable to these relations. Since British ethnic minorities are the subject, the voluminous American literature will be referred to where relevant, but not reviewed in any detail.

It would be wrong to blame the problems of race relations on the attitudes of ethnic minorities. However the psychological response of ethnic minorities to their experience — of immigration, disadvantage and discrimination — is an important part of the whole race relations equation. It can be argued that there are three major barriers to social advance among ethnic minorities. First, they face discrimination. Second, the poor social circumstances in which many blacks and Asians find themselves at present tend to reproduce themselves in the future (even in the absence of discrimination): social mobility is limited for black and white alike. Third, it is often claimed that the discrimination and disadvantage historically experienced by ethnic minorities may be internalised in terms of reduced self-confidence and self-esteem; in this case the removal of present discriminatory barriers may not be enough to permit real social advance on the part of the psychologically damaged social groups. Erikson (1966) for example, in relation to American blacks, has referred to a "widespread and deep-seated inhibition to utilize equality even where it is granted". Much of this paper will be devoted to a discussion of the evidence for the existence of such a third barrier.

The second and third Chapters will discuss the developing attitudes of ethnic minorities during childhood and youth, with specific reference to ethnic pride and self-esteem. Chapter 4 will deal with the role of ethnic minority cultures in the formation of attitudes. Chapter 5 will consider employment aspirations and the debate over how 'realistic' they are. In Chapter 6 the research evidence covering attitudes towards a wide range of public institutions (often concerned with service delivery) will be reviewed, and the specific claim that young blacks are 'alienated' from mainstream institutions will be discussed in that context; attitudes towards the police are dealt with separately in Chapter 7. The penultimate Chapter 8 raises some methodological issues, including that of the limitations of survey-based statistics in this field. The conclusions are presented in Chapter 9.

2 Children

As Pushkin and Veness (1973) point out, it is widely believed that young children in Britain are unconscious of the significance of racial distinctions, and this is apparently borne out by a superficial observation of children of many races playing together at primary school and outside. However, this belief is mistaken. There is a vast amount of evidence, from Britain and a large number of other countries, that children recognise ethnic differences and ascribe social significance to them from very early ages (at 5 years old or even younger).

Doll-studies

Many of the empirical studies examining the racial attitudes of children aged under 10 have followed the procedure used by Clark and Clark (1947), who showed two dolls — identical in every respect except that one was black and one was white — to the black and white children. In these and other studies the children are then asked a number of questions about the dolls such as:— "Which doll are you most like?", "Which doll would you prefer to be?" and "Which is the nicer doll?". The ethnic minority children tend to regard the white doll much more favourably than the white children regarded the ethnic minority doll, as demonstrated by their choice of doll for play and their judgments about which doll was 'nice'. More surprisingly, ethnic minority children more often fail to correctly identify themselves with the dolls of their own ethnic group than do the white children, when asked which doll they resemble. It is argued that the latter result is related to preferences, as young children do not sharply distinguish between what they are and what they wish to be. With increasing age ethnic minority children are more frequently able to identify themselves with the doll of their own colour. Numerous studies carried out in the United States among blacks and whites (reviewed in Pushkin and Veness, 1973), and in New Zealand comparing whites and Maoris (Vaughan, 1964a, 1964b) have produced similar results. The finding appears to be related to the subordinate social status of the ethnic minority group in question. Despite the fact that blacks are in the majority in South Africa, similar differences between black and white children have been discovered there (Gregor and McPherson, 1966). Hong Kong Chinese are in a rather stronger social position than the other ethnic groups mentioned here and of course they represent the majority in Hong Kong. Their children show little tendency to reject their ethnic identity (Morland, 1969).

Milner (1975) conducted a study of 300 West Indian, Asian and white children aged between 5 and 8 attending a number of schools in British cities. The West Indian children were shown a pair of white and black dolls and a pair of pictures representing a black and a white. The Asian children were shown a pair of dolls and a pair of pictures representing an Asian and a white. The white children were shown pairs of dolls and pictures representing whites and whichever immigrant group predominated in their area. The 'dolls' were specially prepared human models rather than commercial dolls. When asked about their *actual* ethnic identity through the question "which doll looks most like you" all the English children chose the white doll, three quarters of the Asian children chose the Asian doll, and only half the West Indian children chose the doll representing a West Indian. When asked about their *ideal* identity ("If you could be one of these two dolls, which one would you rather be?") all the English children, four-fifths of the West Indians and two-thirds of the Asians chose the white doll. Results consistent with these were obtained, expressing a preference for whites on the part of all three ethnic groups, when the children were asked about their preferences for friends and aspirations for future neighbours and companions. Among the ethnic minority children positive evaluations of whiteness went hand in hand with negative attitudes towards their own ethnic group. The West Indian children more often judged the black doll to be the 'bad' or 'ugly' one of the pair of dolls. The Asian children's response was less marked, but three-quarters of them judged the Asian doll to be ugly. The vast majority of the ethnic minority children chose the white doll as the 'nicest' of the pair.

Other research and the effects of increasing age

No research study has attempted to replicate Milner's experiment in children of the same age, although Bagley and Coard (1975) in a sample of 115 black and white children aged 5–10 in London schools showed that the black children had a stronger preference for white skin than white children for black. (The children were asked, if they were to be born again, which colour skin they would prefer). Other research in this field has concerned older children, and has mainly concerned the choice of friends. In this context, we should beware of assuming that a preference for friends of one's own ethnic group is necessarily racist, or that it corresponds to a value judgment that one's own ethnic group is superior to others. While it is difficult to generalise in this field, since each study has a slightly different approach, the balance of evidence supports the view that in-group preferences among ethnic minority children increase with age. The evidence may usefully be summarised in age-group order.

Davey and Mullin (1980) studied 500 black, white and Asian children aged 7–10 from schools in London and West Yorkshire. They found that the Asians and West Indians indicated less preference for their own groups than did whites (although, unlike Milner, there was no evidence of racial misidentification on the part of the minority children). Pollak (1979) reports that black nine-year-olds would prefer black friends. However Richardson and Green (1971), who examined West Indian children aged 10–11 found a preference for light skin colour. In the older age group, stronger in-group preferences are found. Louden (1981) studied the attitude of 375 black, white and Asian adolescents aged 14–16, all of whom were of broadly similar class background, and none of whom had a reading age of less than 10. Louden found that the Asian and West Indian adolescents evaluated their own groups as highly as they did whites. Kawwa (1968) in two studies of London schools found that black children aged 11–17 generally preferred friends of their own group.

More direct evidence emerges from studies by Rowley (1968), Kawwa (1971) and Jelinek and Brittan (1975). Each of these studies showed that, within a sampled group of ethnic minority pupils of various ages, in-group preferences increase with age, particularly during adolescence. The last of these studies was a major survey of 4000 pupils aged 8–14 in multi-racial schools. They found that preference for friends of the same ethnic group increased with age for white, West Indian and Asian children. This was demonstrated both in relation to actual friendships and in terms of desired friendships although, generally speaking, desired friendships evinced less in-group preference than did actual friendships. The pattern of increasing in-group preference among adolescents is therefore fairly well supported.

Interpreting the research findings

Considerable publicity has been given to some of these research findings, particularly those which seem to show that very young children — of all races — prefer representations of whites to those of persons of their own ethnic group. On the face of it, the findings are disturbing, but they need to be interpreted cautiously.

In the first place, they involve presenting children with rather abstract choices different from those they will ordinarily make. "Which skin colour would you like to have?" is a question which it would be difficult to persuade an adult to answer in an unqualified manner. Friendship preference among older children is a much more realistic context. It may be that the very young children in the study are responding to 'darkness' or 'blackness' as symbols associated with evil or the night (with its associated fears). Such responses need not translate directly into racial prejudice in adults. Conversely, the very abstractness of doll-studies may isolate the results from disturbing factors, such as the problems of reciprocity which affect friendship choice. Moreover the wide cross-cultural replication of the doll-studies, and their reinforcement by the childrens' judgments about the 'bad' or 'ugly' doll, suggest that the results are not wholly ephemeral. There have been occasional suggestions that the race of the interviewing researcher prompts the child's response, but most evidence contradicts this view (see Davey and Mullin, 1980).

Secondly, attitudes in general, and racial attitudes in particular, are ill-defined and inconsistent in young children and only gradually become entrenched in the older child. While young children pick up a variety of cultural clues in their environment which they then reproduce, we should beware of assuming that these correspond to deeply held beliefs which will persist into adult life. The ethnic preferences of young children are not at any rate so firmly entrenched that they cannot readily be surmounted by other factors determining preference. Madge (1976) in a study of London children aged between 6 and 8, found that black and white children when unprompted preferred photographs of whites to those of blacks. However, when the children were presented with stories in which adult approval was alternately directed at black and then white children, they tended to endorse the adult approval in their own judgments about the children in the stories. When prompted by adult approval, the black children strongly

5

preferred the black children in the stories. Madge's results underline the importance of the way very young ethnic minority children are treated by adults, since at this stage ethnic preferences are extremely malleable.

3 Older children and self-esteem

'Self-esteem' has been claimed as a "crucial and pivotal concept in analysing race relations. Positions in the social structure are associated with differing degrees of anxiety, self-confidence, and self-esteem, which in turn influence how individuals perceive and behave toward members of different ethnic groups" (Bagley, 1979). A number of measures have been devised to test the self-esteem of an individual on the basis of questionnaire response. The most notable of these has been one developed by Coopersmith (1967). His measure includes 58 items covering self-esteem in the home and family context, self-esteem in school and peer-group, and general evaluation of self.

In a number of research studies reviewed by Bagley, low self-esteem has been found to be associated with prejudiced attitudes to other ethnic groups. Self-esteem is also correlated with educational performance according to research conducted both in Britain and America, and it appears that increased levels of self-esteem both enhance achievement and follow enhanced achievement (Coopersmith, 1975; Bagley, 1979). Parker and Kleiner (1966) and Bagley have cited evidence for the view that low self-esteem among blacks is associated with mental illness.

Ethnic pride and self-esteem

The realisation that one's race or ethnicity commands a lower ascribed social status might well be traumatic. The Clarks (1955) found striking and direct evidence for such trauma. Many of the black children who were asked to identify with one of the black or white dolls, or to colour their own figure in a drawing, were manifestly frightened and upset by the experience. One burst into tears and a number had to be coaxed to finish the tests. In Britain, similarly traumatic responses have been noted by Coard (1971).

If the derogation of a person's skin colour or ethnicity causes them psychological trauma, it would seem reasonable to suppose that this is because it diminishes their self-esteem. Self-esteem is built out of satisfaction with oneself in a number of respects — as loyal friends, good son, mother, lover, worker, leader and so on. These attributes will be weighted in various ways. Diminished ethnic pride will therefore only seriously reduce self-esteem in cases where ethnicity matters to an individual, and carries substantial weight. While this latter assumption is undoubtedly true in most cases, it should not be taken for granted, and its variability deserves a little exploration.

This point reflects a fundamental problem in race relations. Given that two factors together may reduce the self-esteem of an ethnic minority individual — reduced pride in ethnic minority status combined with the attachment of importance to ethnic status — two approaches to the defence of ethnic minority self-esteem present themselves. On the one hand ethnic pride might be increased by emphasising the positive aspects of the ethnic minority community, culture and traditions. On the other hand the essential irrelevance and unimportance of ethnicity might be emphasised: 'colour-blind' policies of 'assimilation' could emerge from this perspective.

It is difficult, if not impossible, to pursue both these approaches simultaneously. They obviously reflect two major strands in thinking about race relations, although the latter 'colour-blind' approach has received much less emphasis in recent years. In part this may be because the importance attached to race and ethnicity is very deeply entrenched. There is a good deal of evidence for this. Madge (1976) for example, found that when children were asked to sort photographs of people into groups as 'the same', more children sorted the photographs on the basis of race than by sex, age, or any other feature. Similar evidence in America led Proshansky and Newton (1973) to assert that "the inescapable reality of colour shades and shadows the Negro child's emerging sense of self, making the development of racial identification an integral part of his total development of self". Coopersmith is more cautious, arguing that "...while 'blackness' may be an underlying aspect of virtually all Negro experience it becomes more or less salient and significant depending on the context in which a given event occurs. Following that line of reasoning such terms as black self-concept and Negro self-esteem appear overgeneralised and are difficult to interpret when situational specifics are not provided".

The attachment of importance to ethnicity cannot be regarded as a universal and invariable condition of humanity. However, if it is difficult to ignore ethnicity, one would expect low self-esteem normally to follow from diminished ethnic pride, and Ziller (1972) and Bagley and Coard (1975) present evidence for this view. However, Hill (1970) found that black male teenagers assessed themselves more favourably than their white counterparts, despite indications that they were rejecting their own colour, and a similar result by Aisthorpe (1976) is reported by Taylor (1981).

Previous claims and the research evidence

Partly on the basis of research studies such as those described in the previous section, it has been widely argued that ethnic minority groups internalise their diminished social status in terms of reduced self-esteem. Claims of this nature were made by Sartre (1960) in relation to Jews in a book first published in 1946, and by Fanon (1968) in relation to blacks in a work first published in 1952. Erikson (1966) claims it as a general result in the social psychology of minority groups. Coopersmith (1975) describes how many American commentators have taken a similar view. In Britain, Coard (1971), for example, has argued that "the Black child is prepared, both by his general life experiences and by the classroom for a life of self-contempt". Similar views can be found in BPPA and Redbridge CRC (1978), and in Pryce (1979).

However, the claim that ethnic minorities have less self-esteem than whites has very often been based on descriptive and impressionistic work, and this is particularly true of work of some years standing. In America more recent empirical studies of children, mainly conducted in the 1970s, have contradicted this view, bringing Coopersmith (1975) to the conclusion that "either the self-esteem of the black child has increased markedly in the past decade or that the inferences gained from observation of 'the black experience' are discordant with and unsupported by more direct evaluation".

In Britain, too, most recent empirical research has contradicted the view that ethnic minorities suffer diminished self-esteem. Hill (1970) found that West Indian adolescents in six schools in the West Midlands evaluated themselves more highly than did whites. Verma (1975), in a study of 306 14–16 years olds in four secondary schools, reports no significant differences in self-esteem as between black, white and Asian pupils. Phizacklea's (1975) study of 78 black and white adolescents showed higher levels of self-esteem among the black sample, although the difference was not statistically significant. Lomax (1977) also found higher levels of self-esteem among the 124 immigrant girls in a London secondary school than among their 194 white counterparts, and Gaskell and Smith (1981) report that blacks esteem themselves no less than whites on the basis of their sample of 244 young blacks and whites aged between 16 and 25. Louden (1981) examined a sample of 375 white, black and Asian adolescents, and found that the ethnic minorities evaluated their own groups as favourably as they did whites. In a study of 635 teenagers aged between 14–19, the DES (1983) found that Asian respondents described themselves about as positively as did whites while the West Indians were rather more positive. There has been only one contrasting result. In a large study of 871 students aged 15–17 in 39 English schools, each black student was compared to two randomly selected whites of the same sex from the same classroom. Blacks of both sexes were found to have lower self-esteem than whites (Bagley, 1979).

There are a number of methodological variations in these studies, quite apart from the difficult problem of conceptualising and operationalising 'self-esteem' through a test questionnaire. One problem is the controls to be applied: is the appropriate comparison between whites and blacks, or between whites and blacks within the same social class? It is not easy to answer such questions finally, not least because the evidence relating social class to self-esteem is equivocal. Most studies of this type simply, but fairly crudely, 'match' the samples of blacks and whites by choosing them from one school or one classroom. The effectiveness of such matching will obviously vary considerably. Louden excluded from his sample those with a reading age of less than ten and those whose father's occupational group was other than from '3' to '5' according to the Registrar General's system of classification. Gaskell and Smith drew their sample of blacks and whites from claimants at one unemployment benefit office, self-help groups and other institutions.

Overall, however, despite Bagley's contrasting evidence, the weight of evidence suggests that young blacks and Asians in Britain esteem themselves as much as their white counterparts (although the evidence on Asians is sparse). In Britain, as in America, we are forced to conclude either that there has been a historical change in the self-esteem of ethnic minorities, or that the experience of ethnic minorities does not lead to reduced self-esteem.

There is certainly some very general evidence for the first possibility. The last few decades have seen quite sharp changes in attitudes toward ethnic minority groups, and in the politics of race relations, combined with a growth in movements which reflect ethnic and racial pride on the part of ethnic minorities. Fanon's (1968) description of the self-denigration and inferiority complex of blacks, published in the early 1950's, has a curiously dated tone. In America empirical evidence has recently been advanced in support of the view that ethnic pride and self-esteem among blacks have increased substantially in recent years. (See for example Hraba and Grant, 1970; Ward and Braun, 1972.) However this explanation can only be tenuous, if only because there are very few empirical studies of ethnic minority self-esteem of more than about fifteen years standing. The empirical studies mentioned above rest their argument for change over time on comparisons with work, such as that by Clark (1955), which examined ethnic preferences and identity in very young children. This is rather different from self-esteem, particularly with respect to older children and adults. Moreover, while the parallels between the United States and Britain in the field on race relations are real enough, they are far from complete. In this connection Bagley and Coard (1975) argue that developments in British race relations lag behind similar events in the United States.

The second possibility is simply that self-esteem among blacks is no lower than among whites. On the face of it, this would appear surprising, given that they face a social environment which ascribes them a diminished social status, and given the evidence discussed in the previous chapter suggesting that as young children, they may aspire to whiteness. One explanation here is that insufficient attention has been given to the later stages in the ethnic minority child's socialisation, when the child comes to terms with his or her own ethnicity, and in-group preferences incease. As Louden (1978) has argued, ethnic minorities are not merely the passive recipients of the majority culture. Older children, in particular, respond actively and critically to the dominent culture, and can adopt strategies which support ethnic pride and self-esteem; young Sikhs may wear turbans, and West Indian youths adopt dreadlocks. On this view, the preservation of self-esteem among ethnic minorities is not dependent on a wholly benign attitude among whites, but rather on an effective response to their social situation by ethnic minorities. Coopersmith, writing of the United States, takes a similar view, emphasising the importance of various psychological defences. When in contact with the white community, he writes, blacks "generally assumed a posture of conformity, although this does not necessarily mean that the self-image of the Black was in accord with and reflective of his action". To the black, such behaviour may appear as wiliness rather than as submissiveness. Such reasoning stands very much in contrast to Proshansky and Newton's (1973) suggestion that "the 'real tragedy' for the American Negro lies in the inferior passive and servile role his is forced to play and more in the fact that he comes to believe in this role".

10

There are some conceptual and methodological problems here. 'Defensive' self-esteem can be regarded as a form of 'false' self-esteem. The braggadocio of the insecure is symptomatic of low self-esteem, but in a questionnaire study it is easy to see how it could appear to represent high self-esteem. The substantial or superficial nature of defensive self-esteem will depend on how firmly it is based. There is a world of difference between the external bravado which covers inner doubts and the reasoned rejection of the lower social status ascribed to ethnic minorities. There are, in addition, a range of intermediate shades.

It is therefore possible to argue that the relatively high self-esteem of ethnic minorities, apparently uncovered by survey research, is at least in part illusory. There is no direct evidence for this, and the questionnaires designed to measure self-esteem attempt to preclude it, but the possibility must be borne in mind.

Self-esteem and ethnic concentration

It is often argued that the level of concentration of an ethnic minority group within a particular area has an important effect on the self-esteem of individuals from that group. However, it is an issue which is difficult to study, since schools and neighbourhoods with a large proportion of ethnic minorities will differ in so many respects from those with a small proportion of ethnic minorities. Davey and Mullin (1980) found few differences between the ethnic preferences of children in low-concentration schools and those of children in schools with a high proportion of ethnic minority pupils, although more black girls in schools where blacks are highly concentrated would prefer to be white. Verma (1975) found no evidence that the self-esteem of black pupils was related to the proportion of blacks in a school. Two further studies support the view that the self-esteem of ethnic minority pupils is affected by the proportion of pupils of their own ethnic group within the school. Louden's (1977) Ph.D. study, reported by Bagley *et al* (1979), found a curvilinear relationship between black adolescent self-esteem and the proportion of blacks in a number of schools in the West Midlands: black self-esteem was highest in the group of schools where there were between 30% and 50% black pupils, and rather lower in the schools where there existed a smaller or larger proportion of blacks. Bagley *et al* (1979) in a major study conducted in 39 British schools, examining the attitudes of some 1,900 pupils between 14 and 16, found a curvilinear relationship between the black proportion in a school class and black self-esteem, but only for males. For girls there was a linear relationship with black girls in the classes with the highest proportion of blacks showing the highest levels of self-esteem.

Overall, the results suggest that where blacks are a very small minority in a school or class, this may damage their self-esteem, perhaps because they feel threatened and heavily outnumbered and lack the social network of support that a larger group would provide. Less distinctly it appears that for males at least, very high proportions of blacks in a school will also reduce self-esteem. These findings, if interpreted more generally, are an interesting sideline on a recurrent debate: is the geographical concentration of an ethnic minority group desirable or undesirable? Does it represent a closely knit mutually supportive community, or an isolated and stignatized ghetto? To speculate a little, the results quoted here suggest that both these points could be correct, although they apply at different levels of ethnic minority concentration. The optimum state may be a community but not a ghetto.

Conclusion

On balance, the evidence suggests that ethnic minorities have levels of self-esteem equivalent to their white peers. If they are psychologically damaged by their experience of British society, there is little direct evidence for it in the field where it has most often been claimed to occur. It follows that we should at least be cautious about explanations of ethnic minority problems which ascribe a major role to some broad psychological or cultural malaise.

That said, there remains an alternative point of view which cannot wholly be dismissed. The largest empirical study carried out in Britain implies that the self-esteem of young blacks *is* lower than that of whites. West Indians appear to under-achieve at school, while Asians generally do not, despite the fact that both groups experience discrimination and disadvantage. This implies that some mediating psychological or cultural factor is at work — and it is known that self-esteem is related to educational achievement. Such an explanation of under-achievement does not rule out any effect of discrimination, given that the experience of discrimination may cause diminished self-esteem in vulnerable groups.

In any case, measures which sustain and increase ethnic pride and the self-esteem of ethnic minorities can be regarded as desirable. This is so partly because the evidence is insufficiently strong to be sure that ethnic minorities do not suffer the damaging consequences of reduced self-esteem, and partly because, in any case, increased self-esteem (which tends to follow increased ethnic pride) seems to have generally desirable consequences, including improved educational performance. In relation to educational policy, this view is endorsed by Taylor (1981) in her review of research into the education of pupils of West Indian origin. If the educational process acknowledges the diverse cultural and ethnic backgrounds of those receiving education and of the population at large this can only be beneficial. If a West Indian child presents a Creole dialect feature it is helpful if it can be recognised as such, rather than merely as 'poor' English. The acquisition of the linguistic and cultural skills necessary to survive in British society should not, and need not, be at the expense of an implicit devaluation of ethnic minority cultures and languages.

4 Culture

This chapter will consider two issues which have received attention in the literature. First, how do the cultural affiliations of young blacks and Asians relate to their socialisation and racial identity. Second, in what sense can the social position of second generation immigrants in Britain be understood as being 'between two cultures'?

Race and cultural affiliation

It has often been pointed out that social scientists have gradually moved from a 'culture' perspective to a 'race' perspective in their understanding of blacks and Asians and their position in Britain. By this it has usually been intended that race is a more fundamental explanatory category, and in particular that the main constraint on life-chances is racial discrimination, rather than problems associated with cultural differences. However, even if this is accepted, it would be wrong to infer that culture has become irrelevant to race relations. Racial factors can affect culture, which in turn will have an effect on perceptions of racial differences particularly in relation to the politics of race.

New Commonwealth immigrants arriving in this country had different cultures, as well as a different racial appearance. The difference of culture was much greater in the case of the Asian than for West Indians. Asians had little or no intention or expectation that they would be rapidly assimilated into ordinary British life following immigration. The distinct form and strength of their cultural and religious traditions, together with their firm ties with kin in the sending country (and the expectation that they would at some point return there), precluded any such possibility. West Indian immigrants were in rather a different position. Their education in the West Indies had taught them to regard Britain as the mother country, and to assume that they showed a common culture with the indigenous population. Acceptance and some kind of assimilation seemed assured.

It is helpful at this point to draw a theoretical work by Tajfel (1981). In a slightly different context, he outlines three possibilities for an ethnic minority group:—

> To sum up: we distinguished between three general sets of conditions which all lead to the appearance or strengthening of in-group affiliations in members of minorities. In the first of these, a common identity is thrust upon a category of people because they are at the receiving end of certain attitudes and treatment from the 'outside'. In the second case, a group already exists in the sense of wishing to preserve its separate identity, and this is further reinforced by an interaction between the 'inside' and the 'outside' attitudes and patterns of social behaviour. In the third case, an

existing group might wish to dilute in a number of ways its differences and separateness from others; when this is resisted, new and intense forms of a common group identity may be expected to appear.

In a previous chapter, the growing preference of ethnic minority adolescents for friends of the same ethnic group was described. It seems highly unlikely that any such increasing preference for one physiognomy over another should occur without a rationalised basis. Cultural preference is an obvious candidate for such a role. In other words, an adolescent's growing preference for his or her own ethnic group is given an intellectual form through preferences for particular styles of behaviour, music, clothes and so on. In this way culture acts as a symbol of race, and the existence of a distinct ethnic minority culture supports racial pride and in turn self-esteem. Bagley and Coard (1975) provide direct empirical evidence for this view. In a study of 131 black and white children aged 5–10, drawn from two London schools, they found that the black children who tend to reject their ethnic identity also tend to know less about their own culture.

The black or Asian teenager may therefore draw on 'culture' to support a positive self-image. An understanding of this process and the rather different ways it occurs among Asians and West Indians, has some relevant implications. First, it may be expected that this process is rather easier for Asians than for West Indians. This is partly because the distinctness of Asian culture lends itself readily to an intellectual foundation for racial pride, and partly because many West Indians — in particular the first generation of immigrants — often expected assimilation into white British society. Milner's work also suggests that rejection of one's own skin colour is more frequent among young West Indian children than it is among Asians. Louden (1981) argues that "In the case of Asians the strong kinship and group reinforcement has insulated them from the harsh and negative reaction of the majority group". Nowikowski and Ward (1979), describing the position of middle class Asians in suburban South Manchester point out how the experience of discrimination acts primarily to *reinforce* existing ethnic ties and commitments. Ballard and Ballard (1977) argue similarly in relation to Sikhs, particularly of the second generation, pointing out that racism has "precipitated a reactive pride in their separate ethnic identity". They add an interesting further observation:—

> Young people are ... gradually moving towards the establishment of an over-arching South Asian ethnic group, while the first generation have tended to organise themselves in terms of the narrow loyalties of their homelands — based on caste and kinship. Although these divisions remain of some importance to the second generation, not so much because of intellectual conviction but rather because of their commitment to their parents, the fact that all young people are reacting similarly to common external constraints is drawing them together.

Second, the in-group preferences and levels of self-esteem equivalent to their white peers which are found in older West Indians teenagers imply that the task of giving a cultural form to enhanced ethnic pride is usually accomplished successfully. West Indian immigrants very often regarded their own culture as

14

part of British culture, or at least as a culture not sharply distinct from that of the 'mother' country. Black adolescents are therefore possessed of a rather limited repertoire of cultural forms in which to clothe their racial pride. This will lead to pressure to add to that repertoire or to further develop and give greater emphasis to existing cultural forms which are distinctively West Indian. Here one might mention the Creole dialect, Reggae music, and Rastafarianism — both as a religion and as a cultural symbol. Moreover this process may involve the rediscovery and re-evaluation of cultural features which were de-emphasized by earlier immigrants who believed that such features might prejudice their chances of acceptance in Britain.

Such a culture is sometimes termed a 'culture of resistance'. Miles (1978) argues that "the symbols and cultural practices of Rastafarianism assist a positive affirmation of blackness for black youth". Troyna (1979) makes a more directly political claim, that "reggae increases black youths' awareness of the racialist tendencies of British society and encourages their retreat into an alternative sub-cultural milieu". Louden (1981) explains the relatively high levels of self-esteem among West Indian adolescents in terms of the 'black power' movement and in the "new-found distinctiveness" which does its job of "creating a positive and healing new version of social identity". The development of such a 'culture of resistance' is a major aspect of the lives of many young blacks in Britain.

Third, the processes described appear to occur in early adolescence, although the evidence is not at all firm on this point, and one may expect much individual variation. Most young adolescents also feel a need to assert their independence from their parents, and will clothe their self-assertion in the sub-cultural styles of their generation and peer-group. The ethnic minority adolescent is therefore faced with the task of simultaneously appealing to ethnic minority culture as a support of racial pride, while also asserting independence from parents. It is no accident that a belief like Rastafarianism is adapted to both tasks. However it is also possible that these simultaneous demands may create psychological conflict, given that in most cases the relevant ethnic minority culture will be that of the adolescent's parents.

A commitment to an ethnic identity can therefore emerge as a defensive response to majority society, as well as from the intrinsic rewards of belonging to an ethnic minority culture. For the reasons outlined above the 'defensive response' is likely to be a more important factor for West Indians — particularly the young — then in the case of Asians.

Between two cultures?

A number of writers have discussed the ethnic identity of immigrants — particularly of the second generation — from the rather different perspective of a 'conflict' between the demands of the ethnic minority cultural mores and those of indigenous British culture. This view has emerged in the much-used phrase 'Between two cultures' which has been used as the title of two publications (CRC, 1976; Watson, 1977). Miles (1978) summarises the point of view (which he rejects) as follows:—

In essence, the argument is that these migrant groups are the victims of 'culture clash' (there being a conflict between their own, or their parents' culture and that of the receiving society), with the result that either their own culture is devalued or its basis or coherence is modified by 'western' influences. This argument is of some practical significance because it can follow from arguing that such minorities are not wholly part of the culture of the country of origin or of the receiving society, that they are 'alienated' outside of two different cultural forms, and that therefore social policies should aim to 'integrate' them.

This view and ones akin to it are relatively common among what might be called 'informed opinion', although the two publications entitled "Between Two Cultures" cannot necessarily be associated with it. However it can be misleading.

First it involves the assumption that a 'culture' is the homogeneous attribute of an ethnic group or nation state. This is an over-simplification. Rex (1982), for example, has underlined the point: "The child of immigrant parents does not merely have to be socialised into some seamless British culture. He enters into a complex process of intergenerational and class conflict in which he will both share experiences with working class and middle class British youth and be divided from them". This is a useful reminder of the manifold quality of 'culture'. We all face difficulty and conflict in moving between the norms and values of the school, the home, the workplace, the pub, the trade union, the church, although we are also conscious of advantages in moving from one social context to another. British 'culture' encompasses the Free Presbyterian crofting communities of the Western Isles, high table at All Souls College Oxford, and adolescent glue-sniffers in South London. Long before the years of New Commonwealth immigration, Britain was already a multicultural society. The cultural divide between Asian immigrants and the indigenous population is different both in form and extent from cultural divisions which exist within the indigenous population, but the Britain in which immigrants and their children appear is a society where cultural diversity and cultural conflict are already endemic.

The second misconception is that the juxtaposition of different cultures necessarily creates problems of 'culture conflict' or 'identity crisis' in persons between two cultures. In part this misconception stems from the first. Given that ordinary social life involves a continuous mixing of cultures, the introduction of an ethnic minority culture does not of itself necessarily demand a very radical social adaptation. Moreover a person placed 'between two cultures' — such as a second generation immigrant — will often find that as many advantages emerge from this position as do problems. Under ideal circumstances such a person can choose the best aspects of each culture. The young Asian woman who rejects an arranged marriage will often be faced with conflict with her parents, but from her point of view she will be taking advantage of the rather different approach to marriage adopted by her white peers. In the context of social work practice, Ahmed (1981) argues that the idea of 'culture conflict' can obscure as much as it explains when working with Asian girls. Persons poised between cultures need

16

not experience 'identity crises', for there is no necessity to make any final existential choice between one culture and another. As Miles points out, "it might be more accurate to speak of the children of immigrants as being *bicultural* rather than between two cultures: the present 'second generation' live their lives in two cultural contexts, adopting by choice, but within identifiable constraints, the most appropriate norm or practice, depending on the circumstances they face".

Among the second generation, there is a risk that generational conflict will be misread as cultural conflict. As has been described, many adolescents reach for a cultural (often sub-cultural) basis with which to form an identity opposed to that of their parents. In the case of ethnic minorities the cultural basis available will often be that of white society, since it will be this culture which is most immediately available. The form of conflict is cultural, but its basis is generational. Ballard and Ballard (1977) emphasize how such conflict can be misinterpreted, and mention that some Asian parents may themselves do so, conceiving their children's wish "for a slightly greater degree of independence as the beginning of a headlong rush into total anglicisation". However, both Ahmed and the Ballards also argue that generational conflict among Asians is often misinterpreted by whites in very ethnocentric terms, as involving excessively authoritarian parents.

17

5 Aspiration and achievement

Unrealistic aspirations?

It is sometimes said that the job aspirations of ethnic minority school-leavers are too high. It can be argued that this will damage their job prospects, since they will be unprepared to accept the lower status jobs which are more likely to be available. An early study by Beetham (1967), conducted in five Birmingham schools, showed that Asian and West Indian boys had rather higher aims and expectations than did white school-leavers, and a few particular jobs, including engineering and work as an electrician, were mentioned very frequently by the ethnic minority school-leavers as desired jobs. West Indian girls did not have much higher job aspirations than their white counterparts, although they were equally limited in variety. Beetham concluded that the immigrants' aspirations were 'unrealistic'. This view was repeated in evidence given by the Youth Employment Service to the Sub-Committee on Race Relations and Immigration (SCORRI, 1969), who continued by arguing that "... so long as they were unwilling to consider other jobs, they are likely to miss opportunities of suitable employment and remain unemployed". Nandy (1969) attacked these views, arguing that the 'realism' of aspirations is an ambiguous notion, and suggesting that the high aspirations of immigrants and their children reflect their realisation that they must aim higher if they are to do as well as whites.

Nandy is right to point out the ambiguities in the label of 'unrealistic aspirations'. An aspiration is a desire, and there is nothing inherently irrational in a desire — say to become a film star — provided there is no accompanying expectation that the desire will be easily fulfilled. Moreover, the question arises of whether a school-leaver's aspiration is 'unrealistic' because qualifications are lacked, or because although the school-leaver has the requisite qualifications, there are very few jobs, or because of racial discrimination. The term 'unrealistic aspirations' slides over these important distinctions, and strongly implies that persons possessed of such aspirations should be less ambitious. This last implication is very questionable. Beetham suggests that the immigrants' greater "ambitions" means that he "is likely to be less easily and happily integrated into the English employment structure". Although this may be true, such ambition may also be necessary for immigrants to obtain occupational advance; we all have to decide whether to rest content with what we have or risk failure by trying for more.

The research evidence

Apart from Beetham's research, two other studies were carried out in the 1960s. Figueroa (reported by the Institute of Race Relations in SCORRI, 1969) compared a sample of West Indian school-leavers with one of English leavers of the same age and the same general level of educational attainment. Like

Beetham, Figueroa found a strong desire among the black school-leavers for a rather narrow range of jobs, particularly engineering jobs for boys. However, he interpreted his results rather differently, as displaying no more than 'modest' job aspirations. One other unpublished study by Bhatnager, also carried out in the 1960s, found no significant differences between the job aspirations of immigrant school-leavers and those of their white counterparts (reported by Gupta, 1977). One interesting if rather tenuous finding is that of Pirani (1974) who asked 20 Asian, 20 West Indian and 20 white fifteen years olds attending a Bristol school to write essays on the subject of "what I would like to be in future and what I think I will be". The white (working-class) children recognised that they often would not get what they wanted, the Asians felt relatively certain that they could achieve their goals, while the West Indian pupils ignored the question of 'what I will be' and concentrated on the 'what I would like to be' part of the question. The West Indian boys also concentrated on a style of life to which they aspired (predominantly involving status possessions such as cars and clothes), rather than on job aspirations. Pirani argues that the white children's aspirations are confined within their class positions.

> The Asian children, too, have well-defined expectations placed upon them: but these were sometimes beyond their abilities and this seemed to cause tremendous anxiety as they were eager to please the adult generation. The nature of the Jamaicans' anxiety was different and more serious, in that whilst their parents had high expectations of them these expectations were rather vaguely summed up in such phrases as 'become educated'; meanwhile they had not accepted such expectations for themselves.

However in the 1960s a large proportion of ethnic minority school-leavers would have had no more than a few years residence and schooling in Britain. Now the vast majority of such school-leavers will have been born in Britain or will at least have been brought up here. The Youth Employment Service (since renamed the Careers Service) had explicitly related its 1969 description of 'unrealistic aspirations' to the newness of immigrants, and it would not be surprising if the aspirations of present day school-leavers of New Commonwealth origin were rather different, given that they will have been educated almost entirely in Britain, and face a very different economic climate.

Most recent research suggests that West Indian school-leavers are no more ambitious than their white working class school-mates, or only slightly more so. Most black males aspire to skilled manual jobs, with a technical and mechanical bias. This finding is reported by the CRE (1978), Rex and Tomlinson (1979), Roberts et al (1981), and Lee and Wrench (1983) in separate surveys. Roberts et al report that black respondents of both sexes were slightly more ambitious. Gaskell and Smith (1982) found the job aspirations of blacks to be similar to those of whites in their sample fo 244 young males. These same studies indicate that black women aspire to respectable white collar and professional occupations, such as secretaries, typists and nurses, but their ambitions are not markedly greater than their white counterparts.

The DES (1983) in their study of about 600 whites, blacks, and Asians aged 14–19 of all social classes report that the main difference between the job aspirations of the three ethnic groups is that blacks, and to a lesser extent Asians, more often aspire to work with their hands than whites. The black and Asian respondents also mentioned the importance of an 'understanding boss' and jobs involving 'helping others' more often than whites. However, there is some evidence that young Asians have rather higher job aspirations than their white counterparts. In a study carried out in Glasgow, Fowler, Littlewood and Madigan (1977) found that about three times as many Asians aspired to professional occupations as did whites. In separate studies of Asian and white school-leavers Brooks found the job aspirations of Asians in Walsall to be higher than their white counterparts, although Singh reports no difference in Leicester (Brooks and Singh, 1978). Gupta (1977) studied 42 Asian pupils carefully matched according to a number of variables with 50 white pupils in two outer London comprehensive schools. He found that Asian boys and girls expressed significantly higher vocational (and educational aspirations) than the whites. It should be noted that this last result may be consistent with that of the DES study. Job aspirations tend to be related to the jobs held by the parents of school-leavers. Given that white parents tend, on average, to have higher status jobs than Asian parents, then if Asian school-leavers have similar job aspirations to whites overall, they are likely to have higher job aspirations than whites with parents of the same socio-economic group.

Unemployment and job satisfaction

We may now turn to the question of whether any higher aspirations lead to unemployment by making black and Asian school-leavers unwilling to accept the less desirable jobs which are available. This is likely to happen only if school-leavers have a naive confidence that their desired job will turn up. In Beetham's (1967) study, three quarters of the white boys, just over half the West Indians and something over one third of the Asians anticipated obstacles in securing their chosen job. Gupta's (1977) study produced almost opposite results, in that many more of the Asians, as compared with whites were 'worried' about obtaining the jobs of their choice. In Gaskell and Smith's study, the black unemployed were just as ready as their white counterparts to acknowledge that getting a good job would be hard. This suggests that black and Asian job aspirations, whether or not they have remained high, have become more 'realistic' in their recognition of obstacles to desirable employment. Smith's (1981) study of the ethnic minority unemployed provides more direct evidence for the adult population. Firstly, he showed that West Indian unemployed men were rather less selective in their search for jobs than were white unemployed men, and that the Asian unemployed were much less so. Secondly, of those unemployed who had found new jobs, a higher proportion of the ethnic minority workers than of whites thought that their new job was worse than the old. The difference between whites and minorities was greatest among young people. Taken together these findings show that ethnic minority workers are more prepared than whites to lower their sights when threatened with persistent unemployment — although of course their ideal aspirations may remain high.

The satisfaction obtained from a job is also related to aspirations, since such satisfaction of often follows the fulfilment of an earlier desire to obtain that kind of work. Smith (1976) in a large sample survey, found that black and Asian men (with the exception of Pakistanis and Bangladeshis) were slightly less satisfied with their jobs than were whites. (Smith interprets the relatively high job satisfaction of Pakistanis and Bangladeshis by suggesting that "their point of reference still tends to be the country of origin".) Among West Indian women, there is some evidence that they are less satisfied with their jobs than whites in the same job (Wild and Ridgway, 1970). However on the evidence of the major survey, the levels of job satisfaction reported by ethnic minority men do not suggest that their aspirations are massively out of step with the jobs which are in fact obtained.

Conclusion

In conclusion, there is good evidence that Asian school-leavers aspire to rather better jobs than do their white schoolmates, and much weaker evidence that the same is true of West Indians. Despite this, it is clear that ethnic minorities on entry into the labour market are prepared to lower their sights in order to avoid unemployment. One claim that is made from time to time is that young blacks are no longer prepared to take the dirty and badly paid jobs which their parents have done in the past, implying that they would prefer to remain unemployed than accept poor jobs. (See for example Dondy (1974).) While this could be so for certain groups of young West Indians, it has yet to show up in aggregated statistics covering their involvement in the labour market.

In this context, the phrase 'unrealistic aspirations' is both ambiguous and misleading, and would be better abandoned. Summing the most recent evidence, Brooks (1983) writes that "we have no reason to suppose that in terms of their abilities, educational qualifications, and potential, the job aspirations of black and Asian youngsters are any more 'unrealistic' than those of their white indigenous peers". In a time when over half of all black school-leavers under 20 are unemployed, the most 'realistic' expectation of a less well qualified black school-leaver will be to become unemployed, (CRE, 1982). There are good reasons why persons placed in such circumstances should hope and try for more than they can probably expect; if self-respect is to be retained, aspirations will necessarily remain out of step with the realities of the labour market.

6 Attitudes to whites and institutions

Earlier sections described how Asian and black teenagers show an increasing preference for members of their own ethnic group as they grow older. It would be wrong to infer that this involves any increase in hostility toward white people. In fact the evidence tends to support the opposite conclusion: an increase in ethnic pride tends to enhance self-esteem, which in turn is linked to racial tolerance. (For a review of the literature on the connection between self-esteem and prejudice, see Ehrlich (1973).)

This result may appear surprising. Coopersmith (1975) points out that high self-esteem has, because of cultural emphasis, been associated with 'arrogance' and 'feelings of superiority'. In fact the research evidence points the other way, indicating that high self-esteem is associated with 'openness', 'friendship' and with self-respect without claims of superiority, or the degradation of others. More directly, Bagley (1979) reports a number of empirical studies conducted in British schools reporting strong correlations between poor self-esteem and racist attitudes. The majority of these studies were conducted on white teenagers using Coopersmith's questionnaire measures of self-esteem and a set of questions designed to measure racist attitudes. A further study by Bagley using a measure of anti-white attitudes found that poor self-esteem was significantly correlated with hostility to whites in a sample of 141 black pupils drawn from 39 schools. The apparently paradoxical connection of self-denigration and hositility was noticed by Foner (1977) in her study of Jamaicans. Writing of a rural Jamaican community, she writes that "although many villagers resented whites' privilege and power and harboured hostility towards them, most still continued to denigrate their own blackness and to believe in the superiority of white skin and white (European) culture". Foner goes on to argue that the racial attitudes of villagers change quite significantly on migration to Britain.

When groups within the ethnic minority communities engage in activities which exclude whites and manifest cultural or racial pride this may be seen as threatening or divisive by the majority community, and as damaging to community relations. Since the evidence suggests that such activities will generally improve self-esteem (and therefore tolerance) on the part of those taking part, any damage to community relations could well be attributable to the response of the white community, rather than to the activities themselves. This is not to say that all groupings of ethnic minorities will be benign, but it is worth noting that Bagley and Verma (1975) in a study of inter-ethnic attitudes, found no evidence that a commitment to black power ideology on the part of West Indians was related to hostile attitudes to whites. This study involved a comparison of the inter-ethnic attitudes of some 200 white, Asian and black teenagers aged 14–16 selected from 12 schools in multi-racial areas of London and the West Midlands. Anti-white, anti-West Indian and anti-Asian attitudes were independently measured. The whites demonstrated the highest levels of hostility towards other ethnic groups. The West Indians and Asians showed more tolerance, although some hostility towards whites emerged, particularly on the part of West Indians. While this review is primarily concerned with the attitudes of ethnic minorities, feelings of racial hostility on the part of blacks and Asians need to be placed in the context of the rather more intense attitudes of whites.

There is a conceptual difficulty here, analogous to that already discussed in relation to ethnic identity. It is open to question how much weight and meaning can be attached to generalised measures of hostile inter-ethnic attitudes. In practice, attitudes will be more ambivalent and more dependent on context than such generalised measures can acknowledge. Ambivalence can emerge in the co-existence of deference with resentment, or of paternalistic affection with faint contempt. Such ambivalence relates to the dependence on context. The idea of a daughter marrying a person of another ethnic group may generate a response very different from that generated by the idea of taking on that same person as an employee. The remainder of this chapter, will therefore consider inter-ethnic attitudes in relation to rather more specific social contexts. That said, social psychological research on the nature of racial prejudice generally supports the view that racial prejudice is a relatively deep-seated personality feature. To that extent generalised measures of inter-ethnic attitudes tell an important part, if not the whole of the story.

Perceptions of discrimination

For obvious reasons, a major determinant of how blacks and Asians relate to whites in Britain will be the former groups' perceptions of racial discrimination and its extent. A small study conducted by Levine and Nayar (1975) found that Asian immigrants generally believed discrimination to occur. In a major survey Smith (1976) found that white and ethnic minority men accepted that discrimination occurs in housing and employment. Asians were generally less aware of discrimination than West Indians — perhaps because of their greater cultural isolation — and Asian men were actually less likely than whites to believe in the occurence of discrimination. Moreover, only a relatively small proportion of blacks and Asians actually claimed personal experience of discrimination, and this proportion was considerably smaller than that which might have been expected to have experienced discrimination, on the basis of research covering its extent. As Smith points out, this is probably due to the fact that most discriminatory practice will not be evident to the unsuccessful applicant for a job.

The more recent 1981 PSI survey of ethnic minorities has produced very similar results although rather more West Indians claimed personal experience of discrimination. However it is surprising that while four-fifths of the West Indian respondents believed discrimination to occur, less than half the Asian respondents did so — a proportion no higher than in 1974 (Brown, 1984). Another sur- of young people aged 16–20 (Anwar, 1982) while broadly supporting the conclusions of the two major surveys, found that over four-fifths of the Asian respondents believed that some employers are racially prejudiced. This suggests that younger Asians now entering the labour market are considerably more aware of discrimination than their parents.

Generally speaking ethnic minorities make a rather modest estimate of the amount of discrimination they experience and many older Asians are even prepared to deny its existence. This contradicts two views advanced from differing political perspectives. Blacks and Asians do not have chips on their shoulders in the sense that they are excessively prone to believing discrimination has occurred when in fact it has not. Equally, they do not perceive their position in employment as one involving a constant and unrelenting struggle against racism; in the 1981 PSI survey, only 11% of ethnic minority respondents believed that *most* employers discriminate (Brown, 1984).

A related question is that of how unemployment affects perceptions of discrimination. Smith (1981), in a survey of the unemployed, found limited indications that unemployment stimulated a greater awareness of discrimination, although very few black or Asian unemployed persons spontaneously blamed their loss of a job on discrimination. Anwar's (1982) study of the young unemployed found rather stronger evidence relating experience of unemployment to the perception of discrimiantion. Young unemployed Asians were nearly twice as likely to think that the majority of employers were racially prejudiced than were Asians in jobs.

Attitudes to institutions

The attitudes of ethnic minorities to statutory and establishment institutions and organisations is a particularly important context in which any hostile feelings towards the 'white' establishment may emerge (given that such institutions are mainly staffed by whites). It is sometimes argued that ethnic minorities, particularly young blacks, are unwilling to use conventional institutions responsible for service delivery. If this were so it would follow that any failure of statutory institutions to meet the needs of blacks and Asians is attributable not only to the quality of service delivered to them and its relevance to their special needs, but also to the negative attitude of ethnic minorities towards the services in question.

Education

The research literature on the attitudes of young British blacks towards education has been reviewed by Taylor (1981). Hill (1968), who interviewed 400 pupils aged 14–15 in six secondary schools, found that West Indians had a generally favourable attitude towards education. Evans (1972) in a study of 150 West Indian youths aged 16–24 in Birmingham obtained a similar result. The major study in the field has been that by Jelinek (1977),who surveyed some three and a half thousand pupils of varying ages and ethnic groups. The attitudes of the West Indian pupils towards school and schoolwork were found to be close to the overall norm. More recent research such as that carried out by Dawson (1978)

24

and Gaskell and Smith (1981a) suggests that if anything, black pupils have more positive attitudes towards schools than do whites. The DES (1983) report that about two thirds of black teenage respondents 'like' school, compared to half the whites; only 5 percent 'dislike' or 'disliked' it, compared to 18 percent of the whites. One way in which such positive attitudes are manifested is through involvement in further education. Black youths are generally more likely than whites to attend such courses (OPCS, 1980).

Asian children also generally manifest positive attitudes towards their school. Jelinek (1977) reports that the Asian children in her sample had the most positive attitude towards school and were the group most concerned about their school work. Gupta (1977), in a study of 92 white and Asian pupils of school-leaving age in two London schools, found that the Asians had a stronger desire to stay on at school than their white counterparts. The DES (1983) found that Asians liked school even more than West Indians, who in turn, as mentioned, like it more than whites.

The reasons for such positive attitudes on the part of ethnic minorities require further exploration. It may reflect the views of parents who in most cases will not have had access to such an education. Alternatively it could be that the alternative to school — entry into the labour market — has fewer attractions for ethnic minorities than whites because of the more serious risk of unemployment borne by young blacks and Asians. This point may particularly apply to the positive evaluation of staying on at school and further education.

Employment services

Attitudes to jobs have already been discussed in Chapter 5. Attitudes towards the employment services provided by the government may now be considered. The Community Relations Commission (1974) interviewed some one hundred 'experts', (Careers Officers, Community Relations Officers, youth workers, teachers and policemen who had experience of working with young blacks). These 'experts' felt that young West Indians 'viewed the Youth Employment Service with cynicism and distrust'. The report also describes the problem of unemployed blacks failing to register at Employment Exchanges and Careers Offices, and many of the experts claimed that young blacks feel the Employment Exchanges are humiliating although they prefer Careers Offices. While the report gives considerable weight to these findings, it is worth noting that the national survey of some 600 young blacks and whites, described in the report, suggests that unemployed young blacks are no less likely to register as unemployed than are similarly placed whites, and the young blacks in the survey had views towards careers offices and employment exchanges which were similar to those of whites. A similar finding is reported by Gaskell and Smith (1981a).

Race relations research will always tend to throw up 'problems' afflicting ethnic minorities. It requires a further step in the agrument to relate such problems to race or ethnic origin rather than to those of inner city youth for example, or of working-class people. This inference is not one to be made lightly since, if it is mistaken, it may lead to a misconception of the problem as being one of race relations, and an equally inappropriate policy response.

In the present context, there is good evidence to show that ethnic minorities use employment services at least as much as do whites. The CRC study just described obtained this result. Smith (1976) reached similar conclusions on the basis of the major 1974 survey of ethnic minorities conducted by PEP. Dex (1979), analysing data on school-leavers in Bradford and Sheffield collected in 1972 and 1973, found that nearly two thirds of the West Indians obtained their first jobs through school or the Youth Employment Service compared with just over half the Asians, and rather under half the whites. The use of these services by West Indians fell drastically in relation to their second and third jobs after leaving school, and as Dex points out, their initial heavy use of the statutory services is likely to reflect as much their lack of word-of-mouth contacts as it does their satisfaction with statutory provision. Most recently Anwar (1982), in a survey of about one thousand 16–20 year olds in inner city areas, found that black and Asian youths seek and find jobs through job centres, employment offices and school just as frequently as whites. Equally, there is good evidence to show that unemployed blacks and Asians register as unemployed just as frequently as whites. The CRC (1974) itself provided data in support of this conclusion. Smith (1976) reports a similar result from the PEP Survey. Field *et al* (1981) surveying the evidence from the 1966 Census, the 1977 Labour Force Survey and the 1977–78 National Dwelling and Housing Survey are in agreement. A special survey of 550 16–20 year olds and the recent CRE survey reinforce the point (Roberts *et al*, 1981; Anwar, 1982). The evidence could not be stronger: if there is a problem of unregistered unemployment it is not related to race.

'Alienation'

Research by Gaskell and Smith (1981a) on some 250 black and white males aged 16–25 has provided further support for the view that young blacks have quite positive views towards many features of British society. The sample was specifically chosen so as to include those who might be thought to be most distanced from mainstream British institutions. It was drawn from the unemployed registering at one benefit office, from further education colleges, from employers, a youth club and from among black attenders of self-help groups. The sample was not strictly random, but was broadly comparable with the general black and white population of young males. The black respondents were found to have positive attitudes towards newspapers, educational institutions, job centres and careers offices; they were more neutral about employers, television, and British people, and negative about politics in Britain and the police. Although the black respondents manifested considerable hopelessness and despair, they were generally *more* positive about British institutions than were respondents in the white sample. These are striking results, particularly given that 'black male youth' is the group from within ethnic minority communities which is frequently assumed to be most hostile to British institutions. Sharma (1980) found rather similar results in relation to Asian adolescents in Britain.

26

Gaskell and Smith also set themselves to consider whether or not black youth is really 'alienated'. This view of 'alienated black youth' has become something of a cliché over the last decade, and the term 'alienation' has gradually intruded into the race relations literature, often without clear definition or relation to earlier notions of 'alienation' in the sociological literature. Stevenson and Wallis (1970) in an article entitled 'Second generation West Indians: a study in alienation' simply describe various forms of racial disadvantage under the heading of 'alienation'. Bagley (1975) defines alienation (in particular relation to West Indians) "... as a failure, because of factors in social structure, to reach the normal goals to which an actor is motivated". Again this amounts to little more than a synonym for racial disadvantage (or at least to that portion of it attributable to discrimination), particularly as Bagley continues by indicating that 'normal goals' involve "reaching the material levels (in terms of occupation, income and housing) enjoyed by the majority of the population". The CRC (1974) report on Unemployment and Homelessness also used the term. Their panel of 'experts' agreed that 'young blacks are likely to become alienated from society'. 'Alienated' was not defined, but was associated with unemployment, suspicion of official bodies and despair. This report led, in particular, to the view that certain unemployed or homeless young blacks, by virtue of their alienation, were beyond the reach of the normal social services. This was most explicit in the original rationale for the CRE's self-help scheme (Fisher and Joshua, 1982). However there was never any real evidence for this last view. Roberts, Duggan and Noble (1981), in an examination of unregistered unemployment among blacks and whites point out that "non-registrants attitudes, job aspirations and preferred life-style often turns out to be thoroughly conventional", and deny that non-registrants are in any sense 'alienated'. Gaskell and Smith concur; if alienation is interpreted in terms of negative attitudes to establishment institutions, white youths are, if anything *more* alienated than similarly placed blacks.

Of course it can always be argued that researchers have failed to pick up 'alienated' black youths precisely because they are alienated, and therefore difficult to reach by statutory institution and researcher alike. However at some point, as with unreported crime, some evidence must be advanced for their exist-ence and extent. None has been forthcoming in relation to 'alienated black youth'. Gaskell and Smith conclude that 'alienation' is a quite unhelpful notion with which to understand the problems of black youth. Given that the term is either redundant or else positively misleading, their view can only be endorsed.

Conclusion

The main conclusion of this section is that ethnic minorities in general, and young blacks in particular, are no more hostile to establishment institutions than are whites. (Attitudes to the police are an exception to this pattern and this will be discussed in the following section.) It would be wrong to infer that these institutions are wholly effective in meeting the special needs of ethnic minorities, or indeed that blacks and Asians are uncritical of the services provided. John

(1972) for example found that while the West Indian teenagers in his study had a relatively positive attitude towards school in general they were critical about what they had learned at school and over the type of jobs to which their schooling would lead. Such practical criticism, however, is very different from fundamental emotional and cultural opposition to establishment institutions.

7 Attitudes towards the police

Ethnic minorities tend to express more criticism of the police than do whites. Evans (1971), in a survey of 450 young males from Southall, Bradford and Handsworth, found that two thirds of the young West Indians believed that the police deal unfairly with their own ethnic group, compared with less than one third of the Indians and Pakistanis. The CRC (1974) in a national survey of black and white persons under 25 reported that nearly 80% of the blacks agreed with the statement that "Around here, the police often pick on black people". Ratcliffe (1981) in a survey of Handsworth youths living at home with their parents reports that two thirds of the Asians, but only one quarter of the West Indians, believed that the police treat black people fairly. Southgate (1982) in a study of 532 males aged 15–35 found that West Indian and Asian witnesses of the 1981 Handsworth riot rated police behaviour less favourably than did white onlookers. In a survey of 600 14–19 year olds conducted by the Department of Education and Science (1983), more than half of the West Indian respondents stated a belief that the police singled their group out, compared with less than one sixth of whites and Asians in respect of their ethnic groups. Some previously unpublished findings from the British Crime Survey may also be reported here. 30% of black respondents reported themselves to have been 'annoyed' with police behaviour during the previous five years, compared to less than half that proportion of whites and Asians. Similarly, one third of the whites, one quarter of the Asians, and one fifth of the blacks believed that the police did a 'very good job' in the area. Some two thirds of white respondents, just under half the Asians and about one third of the blacks felt that the police understood the problems of their area. (For further details of the British Crime Survey, see Hough and Mayhew, 1983). Stevens and Willis (1981) found that black people, and to a lesser extent Asians, are much more likely to complain against the police than are whites.

A recent major survey by the Policy Studies Institute, carried out in London, has produced a great deal of information about the attitudes and experience of whites and ethnic minorities in relation to the police (Smith, 1983). A sample of 2420 persons aged 15 or over was used, and within this sample the representation of ethnic minorities and young people was substantially boosted. The results from this survey corroborate, in broad terms, those which have just been described. Nearly two thirds of West Indians, and just over one third of Asians felt that some groups were unfairly treated by the police, compared to one quarter of whites.

One study conducted in the Moss-Side area of Manchester (Tuck and Southgate, 1981) has produced slightly different results. In their survey of 750 blacks and whites they report that in the youngest age group (16–24), no more West Indians

29

than whites expressed criticism of the police — about one third of each group. Although older people were generally less critical, older West Indians were more prepared to criticise the police than were older whites. Smith's recent study supports the view that younger people of all ethnic groups are more critical of the police. He found that while there was little variation in attitude up to age 44, people aged 45 or more were much less likely to think that any groups are unfairly treated by the police. The ethnic minority population of Britain is a young population, and this partly explains their more critical attitude. However, with the exception of Tuck and Southgate's study described above, most studies have shown that, even among the young, West Indians and Asians are more critical of the police. Smith reports that among Londoners aged 15–24, more than two thirds of West Indians and just over half the Asians felt that some groups do not receive fair treatment, compared with two fifths of their white counterparts.

One other possibility is that ethnic minorities are less favourably disposed towards the police because of their occupational status. However Smith found that considerably more persons in the professional and managerial groups felt that the police treated certain groups unfairly than was the case among the lower socio-economic groups, although the unemployed were substantially more critical of the police on this point, and unemployment disproportionately affects both young workers and ethnic minority workers.

To sum up, ethnic minorities appear more critical of the police than whites. Factors such as youth and unemployment partially, but rarely wholly, explain this position. Moreover, the review of research in the previous section demonstrated that ethnic minorities are not, in general, hostile to establishment institutions. Therefore if blacks and Asians are more hostile to the police than are whites, it is difficult to explain this in terms of a very general hostility to 'white authority', for such an attitude does not appear to exist. Identifying the reason for hostility towards the police is obviously important, although it is outside the scope of this review. The simplest explanation would relate hostility to personal experience of police attention. However Small (1983) in his study of a group of young blacks in London argues that direct personal experience alone cannot account for attitudes towards the police.

The attitude of Asians towards the police appears, from a number of studies noted above, to be less critical than that of West Indians. Smith's (1983) study supports this view, and also illuminates the differing nature of Asian criticisms. He reports that Asians were actually less likely than whites to believe the police guilty of various kinds of misconduct (including threats, violence, fabricating evidence and accepting bribes) whereas West Indians were much more so. However younger Asians were almost as ready as whites to believe in the frequency of such misconduct. Evans (1972) found that of those young Asians who felt unfairly treated by the police nearly 20% gave as their reason that the police pay no attention to complaints made by their group. Only one of the 95 young West Indians who felt unfairly treated gave the same reason. In the context of racial attacks, Asians have been critical of the level of police protection they receive (Home Office, 1981). Asians may therefore be concerned with the quality of police service to them as much as with their experience of the police as suspects or offenders.

The same point applies to the West Indian community. Smith shows that in London West Indians, together with whites and Asians, believe that catching criminals should be the priority of the police. Tuck and Southgate report from Moss-Side the "considerable usage of and satisfaction with the police by people of West Indian origin in a high-crime inner city area; usage and satisfaction levels not markedly different from those of their white neighbours" (although Smith reports rather less usage of police services by West Indians in London). Some American research (McCaghy, 1968; Campbell and Schuman, 1968) has shown that black citizens who were critical of the police were often as concerned with the inadequacy of police service to their community as with police brutality.

One further and practically relevant measure of attitudes towards the police are views which are expressed on ethnic minorities in the police force and on joining the police.

Anwar (1982) in a survey of 621 persons in 11 inner-city areas carried out immediately after publication of the Scarman report found that over three quarters of blacks and a similar proportion of Asians agreed that more police should be recruited from the ethnic minority community. Even in Brixton, nearly three quarters of black respondents agreed. Smith reports that about one third of Londoners believe that the recruitment of black and Asian police officers will result in the police doing a better job, while between half and two thirds of them think it will make no difference. Very few believed that it would lead to the police doing a worse job, and there was little difference in these findings for West Indians, Asians and whites.

In an unpublished study by MIL Research, prepared for the Central Office of Information, 111 male West Indians aged 16–24 were interviewed and the results compared with those obtained from a much larger sample of whites. Nearly 80% of the young blacks said that they would not consider joining the police force, compared with just over 60% of the whites. Interest in joining the police force was about half as great among the West Indians as among the whites — but it was far from totally absent. The West Indians mentioned many of the same factors as whites when asked about a job as a policeman, but also referred to colour prejudice and the fear that they would lose their friends if they became policemen. Smith's recent survey has corroborated these findings. He reports that in London 10% of Asians and 13% of West Indians between the ages of 15 and 44 have considered joining the police force, compared with 20% of their white counterparts. Saeed and Galbraith (1982) report that just over one third out of 100 (mainly male) teenage Asian schoolchildren interviewed in Croydon schools would agree to be a police officer if the job were offered. These studies together show that while individual blacks and Asians are more reluctant than whites to come forward as potential recruits, there are still a considerable number of blacks and Asians who would like to join the police force, and their recruitment would generally be welcomed in the ethnic minority and white communities.

8 Statistics and lifestyles

The vast majority of research studies reviewed in this paper involved selecting samples from the relevant black, white and Asian populations and asking the selected group a set of questions. This technique of the questionnaire survey is central to empirical social science, and rightly so, but it does have real limitations worthy of scrutiny in relation to the sociology of race.

The surveys reported here often proceed by computing an *average* measure of — say — self-esteem, or in-group friendship preference, or job aspiration, for a particular ethnic group. Such average measures need a little care in their interpretation, for there is a risk that they will provide a stereotyped picture of a 'typical' member of that group. Such average measures cannot do justice to the wide variety of attitudes which exist among the various members of an ethnic group. Explanations which are given for an 'average' attitude are also impoverished. They cannot account for the many different psychological and social strategies adopted by different individuals in the face of similar social circumstances. This point is pressing in the context of race where a peculiarly contradictory psychological logic obtains. For example, one black person, in the face of social circumstances which denigrate blackness, may try simply to keep his head down, to de-emphasize cultural practices which underline his difference from whites and, in general, to adopt a strategy of 'if you can't beat them join them'. Another black placed similarly might challenge the denigration of blacks, insisting proudly on his racial and cultural distinctness. An average attitudinal measure applied to these two individuals would lead to a misunderstanding of both strategies.

Questionnaire surveys are not inevitably hamstrung by this difficulty. All kinds of statistical techniques are available to identify and separate different sub-groups from within a sampled population, so that different patterns of response presented by the sub-groups are not crudely aggregated. Unfortunately the use of these more sophisticated techniques generally involves larger samples and lengthier questionnaires. While it is very much to be wished that further research in the field will experiment with quantitative techniques designed to describe and identify the different psychological strategies open to members of an ethnic minority group, it is likely that much of the empirical evidence will remain, for practical reasons, in the form of average measures. Provided that they are subject to the qualifications made above, such measures will continue to be of great value.

More qualitative forms of research also have much to offer. Rex (1982) has argued the case in a slightly different context. Writing of his own work on West Indian and Asian youth, he concludes:—

The research to which it points is not towards simple cross-tabulations of life-chances and social conditions so dearly loved by British empirical sociology, but to the collection of structured life histories to see how far these ideal types or stereotypes actually reflect the range of empirical reality.

There is of course a great deal of more qualitative and theoretical work (including that of Rex himself) which bears on attitudes. It has not been discussed here since on the one hand it is very difficult to isolate views about attitudes from a more general theoretical perspective, and the attempt to do so will tend to distort the material, and on the other hand the primary concern has been with the empirical evidence which directly relates to the attitudes of ethnic minorities.

One line of research might be mentioned in passing, since it has usefully underlined the variety of strategies open to ethnic minorities accommodating themselves to life in Britain. Pryce (1978, 1979) and Troyna (1979) have grouped West Indians in Britain into different categories according to their 'lifestyles'. Pryce's (1978) definition of lifestyle relates it closely to attitudes, and "to the ways in which individuals in the West Indian community make sense of their world". It is therefore especially relevant to this report. Pryce's (1979) book provides a vivid description of the lives of West Indians living in the St Pauls area of Bristol, and it provides a powerful contrast to the opacities of much survey based research. Pryce describes six life-style groups: 'hustlers, teenyboppers, proletarian respectables, saints, mainliners and in-betweeners'. Hustlers are mainly male and involved in petty crime and prostitution. Teenyboppers are young males who are often homeless or unemployed; they are often involved in Rastafarianism. Proletarian respectables are conventional wage earners who form the bulk of the adult population. Saints are similar, except that their lives revolve around the Pentecostalist faith and they are non-political. Mainliners are better-educated white-collar workers. They are concerned with their social status in white society, and often appear as self-appointed community leaders. In-betweeners, usually in their twenties, are politically conscious individuals who share a law-abiding orientation with mainliners, saints and proletarian respectables, but also share an interest in 'black culture' with hustlers and teenyboppers. Pryce groups proletarian respectables, mainliners and saints as sharing a 'stable law-abiding orientation' aligned with the official values of English society. Hustlers and teenyboppers share an 'expressive-disreputable orientation' in conflict not only with white society but also with West Indian law-abiders. Troyna (1979) in an interview study of black male school-leavers has proposed a simple classification for black teenagers: 'mainstreamers, compromisers and rejectors'. Mainstreamers are 'engaged in reducing the salience of their blackness as a social identity' aiming instead at assimilation. Rejectors are retreating further into those areas of the black community which allow them to define their blackness in positive terms' are often involved in Rastafarianism and are particularly attuned to the political messages of Reggae music. Where main-streamers downplay the extent of racial discrimination, rejectors generally insist on its endemic quality. Compromisers oscillate between these two perspectives. Troyna argues:

I have also tried to dispel the notion that black youth culture is a

33

monolithic and undifferentiated entity ... Faced with 'endemic racialism' these youths develop various adaptive responses. Some certainly do assert their blackness and are assuming less conciliatory responses to the wider society than, say, many of their parents. On the other hand, many young blacks — and particularly those who are successfully negotiating entry into the wider society — are engaged in a process in which a drastic de-emphasis of their black identity is taking place.

Troyna's distinctions, and to a lesser extent those of Pryce, echo and qualify themes in the earlier part of this paper. In Chapter 2 evidence from doll studies, such as that by Milner, was discussed; it implies that very young ethnic minority children may deny their own ethnic status. Older children show an increasing preference for their own group. The work of Troyna and Pryce gives a further dimension to this developmental process, by illustrating how the attitudes of ethnic minority teenagers of the same age may reflect a variety of different responses to their experience.

9 Conclusion

Ethnic minorities in Britain do not lack self-respect, and it makes little sense to speak of the second generation as 'between two cultures', or to claim that ethnic minorities have unrealistic employment aspirations. In general they are not hostile to mainstream British institutions, and 'alienated black youth' has become a misleading cliché. They are not excessively prone to attribute career failure to discrimination, and while they are critical of the police, they are also appreciative of the services they can provide. They are less hostile to whites than whites are to them, and the 'black power' political perspective does not appear to be related to hostility towards whites. In summary, the attitudes of ethnic minorities are very different from those which are often attributed to them, and in many respects are very similar to those of whites. Where attitudinal differences have been found, as with the police, it tends to be the exception and not the rule, and for that reason such differences are unlikely to relate to more general cultural or psychological attributes of ethnic minorities.

[handwritten margin note: it must d since it p inion around white racism; exploita of & colonialism]

Why have traditional views concerning black and Asian attitudes so often been seriously mistaken? In the first place, race relations is an intensely political topic, and this constrains the claims which are made. Gaskell and Smith (1982) make the point as follows:

> The right see the blacks as work-shy, unwilling to accept authority, unable to integrate into British society and predisposed to criminality, while liberals view alienation as a consequence of discrimination, prejudice and the high levels of deprivation, particularly in employment and housing, experienced by many blacks.

Both political perspectives imply that blacks have a rather special set of attitudes and this is reflected in the judgments that are made. Such judgments, in the many cases where they have been mistaken, have been blinkered to a number of factors. First, the cultural differences between whites and people originating from the New Commonwealth do not necessarily result in equivalent differences in attitudes in relation to school, employment and other institutions and practices (at least when such attitudes are conceived broadly, as in the present review). It is notable that in fields where attitudes have been found to be different, those of West Indians are generally more distinct, while Asians have the more distinct culture. Secondly, as a number of previous commentators have emphasised, no one should underestimate the capacity of ethnic minorities to resist, at least at the psychological level, the lower social status they are ascribed.

More generally, researchers working within the perspective of race relations may misperceive any problems thrown up by their research as having their origins in race relations rather than in some other social practice or formation. By doing so

35

they can claim a kind of theoretical ownership over the problem in question. On occasions this can lead to an inverted explanatory framework, whereby similarities between whites and ethnic minorities, rather than dissimilarities, are seen as requiring explanation. Sharma (1980) found that there were no significant differences between the attitudes of Asian adolescents towards trade unions, general elections, taxation, the law courts, and marriage, and the equivalent attitudes of their white counterparts. The reason for these similarities is then posed as a 'question', and it is answered in terms of the relative unfamiliarity of adolescents with such institutions. This is plausible enough, but there is also a simpler possibility; that whites and Asians, given familiarity with the institutions in question, would adopt similar attitudes towards them. To assume otherwise on an a priori basis is to indulge in a form of special pleading for a race relations perspective in social science.

Finally, there is always some tendency, when faced with a social problem, to 'simplify' that problem by referring it to the attitudes of a particular social group, whether it be the 'excessive caution' of civil servants, the 'insularity' of academics, or the 'dogma' of politicians. By virtue of their social position (or the processes involved in their selection), particular groups do often have distinctive attitudes, which obviously play an important role. However such attitudes are very often as much the product of a given social situation as its cause, and the explanation of a social problem in terms of a stereotyped judgment about the psychology of a particular group can, at worst, amount to a refusal to explore any more fundamental causes of the problem in question.

Lawrence (1982) has taken this argument some stages further. He argues that the sociology of race relations can become a theoretical cover for racist ideas, and in particular for blaming the problems of race relations on ethnic minorities themselves. Lawrence criticises the view that West Indians have suffered psychological damage, an impoverished culture, and a weakened family structure as a result of their historical experience of slavery — views put most influentially by Moynihan (1965). He argues that an exclusive or exaggerated emphasis on factors of this sort only shifts attention from the role of present institutions in causing the difficulties of ethnic minority groups and fails to acknowledge their capacity to respond positively and defensively to their historical experience. He claims that much conventional sociology of race relations is ethnocentric and often based on pseudo-psychology.

While Lawrence's argument undoubtedly gains support from the range of opinionated and often unsupported claims which have been made about the attitudes of blacks and Asians, he carries the argument too far.

In the first place it is useful to distinguish between the impact of historically remote social mores and institutions (such as that of slavery) and that of present institutions. Lawrence's point is most applicable to the former effect since any emphasis given to it will tend to shift responsibility from present society (although it must be said that the Moynihan report was a call for remedial action). Where present institutions are concerned, the position is very different: for example, if the achievement of West Indians in school is detrimentally affected by the negative expectations of teachers, then an examination of the social psychology behind this process is of manifest relevance. Research of this type cannot be opposed a priori as 'blaming the victim'. Secondly, Lawrence's insistence on the active and critical response of ethnic minority groups to the culture of the dominant society may be a useful corrective to viewpoints which ascribe a purely passive role to ethnic minorities, but it does not tell the whole story. Ethnic minorities, like everyone else, are neither impermeable to the ideas of the majority nor unresistant to them, and the research reviewed here reflects some of the forms which permeability and resistance take. Lawrence's belief that ethnic minorities have emerged unscathed from their historical experience and are wholly capable of resisting any ideas of the majority group betrays a wish that the moral drama of race relations should be played out with simple heroes and villains, and that the heroes should struggle manfully against all odds, never despairing or becoming embittered. The real world lacks that simplicity.

There remain some real differences between the attitudes of blacks and Asians and those of whites. Blacks, and to a lesser extent Asians, are more hostile to the police than their white counterparts, and this is a subject worthy of further research. There is some evidence that very young ethnic minority children may prefer white to black or brown skin. Although these results are not easy to interpret, they suggest, disturbingly, that derogatory attitudes towards ethnic minorities are sufficiently pervasive to enter the psychological lives of children at a very early age. The role of nursery and primary schools must be important in this context, both in ensuring that such attitudes are not endorsed within the school and in combatting them when they are learnt outside the school.

In older children preference for friends of the same ethnic group increases, and most evidence indicates that black and Asian teenagers esteem themselves no less highly than whites. However one large and fairly systematic study has given a contrary result for blacks, and this might be argued to relate to educational underachievement. Much of the research in this field has applied a rather limited range of controls, and further work in the field would be more illuminating if controls were applied at least for the socio-economic status of the children involved.

The content of the curriculum may have a role to play here. One research study has correlated cultural knowledge with a positive attitude to ethnic identity. Other work has demonstrated that the value judgments made by teachers are extremely influential in the formation of childrens' ethnically related attitudes, and it may be that the curriculum is important mainly because it can appear to invole an implicit value judgment in favour of whites, by teaching about Britain and about the English language. Such value judgments are not inevitably included even in a curriculum which gives a high priority to the skills and knowledge necessary to survive and prosper in British society, and they can be avoided by ensuring that the languages and cultures of the ethnic minority communities receive an appreciative recognition in the classroom, even where they are not directly taught.

Research related to the academic performance of ethnic minorities may have an importance which goes beyond the (sometimes limited) relevance which school qualifications have to future career prospects. There is a sense in which the classroom is a microcosm and a precursor of the wider social world in which ethnic minority youth will seek to prosper. If black underachievement is caused by such factors as diminished ethnic pride and self-esteem (rather than by factors more specifically related to schooling), it would not be surprising if such factors also caused underachievement in the course of working life.

However most evidence implies that black and Asian teenagers esteem themselves as highly as do whites. To achieve this they appear to have overcome an earlier tendency to reject their own ethnic identity. Their defensive response to early socialisation seems to be successful, but it may have hidden costs, at least for racial harmony. If self-esteem is supported through a critical response to earlier experience of whites derogating blacks and Asians, it would not be surprising if that self-esteem were accompanied by hostility toward whites. Some writers have argued this case in connection with the 'culture of resistance' among young blacks, and that a retreat into separatist sub-cultures supports self-esteem but also involves hostility towards whites. It would however be perverse to give much emphasis to ethnic minority hostility toward whites when whites appear to be rather more hostile to blacks and Asians.

Alternatively, a more optimistic view can be put. There is good social psychological evidence to show that high self-esteem is connected with racial tolerance, and strategies which increase self-esteem are therefore to be welcomed as supporting harmonious race relations. For this reason separatist movements which embrace ethnic minority cultures as a means of increasing self-esteem may actually improve relationships with the white community, at least insofar as the quality of such relationships lies in the hands of ethnic minorities.

In practice of course, it is not possible to make global judgments here. Each political and cultural commitment on the part of ethnic minorities will have different implications for self-esteem and for inter-racial attitudes. If British society is to achieve harmonious race relations accompanied by social justice, it must be able to offer ethnic minorities some third alternative apart from cowed deference or self-confident hostility, surrender or battle. The former argument given above would fully apply only in cases where no such third alternative exists, and some have argued that it applies to young blacks. The latter argument demonstrates that at least the social psychological basis for such a third alternative exists.

The future of the ethnic minority communities in Britain depends in part on their own cultural and community resources and on their energy; in part it depends on the nature of the obstacles of their social advance. One such obstacle would arise if ethnic minorities were psychologically damaged by their disadvantaged social position in such a manner that their attitudes themselves become barriers to social advance. Most of the evidence discussed here has run contrary to this point of view. To that extent, the general conclusion to this report must be one of the qualified optimism. However it also focusses attention on the other two obstacles

38

however

Strike out

mentioned originally as fundamental to the life chances of present and future generations of ethnic minorities. The first obstacle is racial discrimination. The second, much less frequently cited, but at least as important, is limited social mobility; all persons in the social groups in which many of the ethnic minorities find themselves — residing in the inner cities, relatively poorly qualified, and with little experience in the type of employment where jobs are more plentiful — have only limited prospects of social and economic advance. Ethnic minorities share such prospects.

References

Ahmed, S. (1981) 'Asian girls and culture conflict'. In Cheetham, J. (Ed.) *Social and Community Work in a Multiracial Society.* London: Harper and Row.

Aisthorpe L. A. (1976). *The Black Child in the Primary School: attitudes and performance.* B. Ed. thesis. Manchester College of Higher Education.

Anwar, M. (1982a). *Young People and the Job Market — A Survey.* London: CRE.

Anwar, M. (1982b). 'Public reaction to the Scarman report'. *New Community* 9, 3, pp. 371–373.

Bagley, C. (1975). 'Sequels of alienation: a social psychological view of the adaptation of West Indian immigrants in Britain'. In K. Glaser (Ed.) *Case Studies on Human Rights and Fundamental Freedoms* vol. 2. The Hague: Nijoff.

Bagley, C. (1979). 'Self-esteem as a pivotal concept in race and ethnic relations'. In Marrett, C. B. and Leggon, C. (Eds.) *Research in Race and Ethnic Relations* vol. 1. Connecticut: Jai Press.

Bagley, C. and Coard, B. (1975). 'Cultural knowledge and rejection of ethnic identity in West Indian children in London'. In Verma, G. K. and Bagley, C. (Eds.) *Race and Education Across Cultures.* London: Heinemann.

Bagley, C. and Verma, G. K. (1975). 'Inter-ethnic attitudes and behaviour in British multi-racial schools' in Verma, G. K. and Bagley, C. (Eds.) *Race and Education Across Cultures.* London: Heinemann.

Bagley, C., Mallick, K. and Verma, G. K. (1979). 'Pupil self-esteem: a study of black and white teenagers in British schools'. In Verma, G. K. and Bagley, C. (Eds.) *Race, Education and Identity.* London: Macmillan.

Ballard, R. and Ballard, C. (1977). 'The Sikhs'. In Watson, J. L. (Ed.) *Between Two Cultures: migrants and minorities in Britain.* Oxford: Blackwell.

Beetham, D. (1967). *Immigrant School Leavers and the Youth Employment Service in Birmingham.* London: Institute of Race Relations.

BPPA and Redbridge CRC. (1978). *Cause for Concern: West Indian pupils in Redbridge.* Redbridge: Redbridge Community Relations Council.

Brooks, D. (1983). 'Young blacks and Asians in the labour market: a critical overview'. In Troyna, B. and Smith, D. (Eds.) *Racism, School and the Labour Market.* Leicester; National Youth Bureau.

Brooks, D. and Singh, K. (1978). *Aspirations versus Opportunities: Asian and white school-leavers in the Midlands.* Walsall CCR and Leicester CRC.

Brown, C. (1984). *Black and White Britain: the third PSI survey.* London: Heinemann.

Campbell, A. and Schumann, H. (1968). 'Racial attitudes in fifteen American cities'. In *Supplemental Studies for the National Advisory Commission on Civil Disorders.* Washington DC: Government Printing Office.

Clark, K. B. and Clark, M. P. (1947). 'Racial identification and preference in Negro children'. In Newcomb, T. M. and Hartley, E. L., (Eds.) *Readings in Social Psychology.* New York: Holt, Rinehart and Winston.

Clark, K. B. (1955). *Prejudice and Your Child.* New York: Beacon Press.

Coard, B. (1971). *How the West Indian Child is Made Educationally Subnormal by the British School System.* London: New Beacon Books.

Community Relations Commission. (1974). *Unemployment and Homelessness: a report.* London: HMSO.

Community Relations Commission. (1976). *Between Two Cultures.* London: CRC.

Coopersmith, S. (1967). *The Antecedents of Self-Esteem.* San Francisco: Freeman.

Coopersmith, S. (1975). 'Self-concept, race and education'. In Verma, G. K. and Bagley, C. (Eds.) *Race and Education Across Cultures.* London: Macmillan.

Davey, A. G. and Mullin, P. N. (1980). 'Ethnic identification and preference of British primary school children'. *Journal of Child Psychology and Psychiatry* 21, 3, pp. 241–251.

Dawson, A. L. (1978). 'The attitudes of black and white adolescents in an urban area'. In Murray, C. (Ed.) *Youth in Contemporary Society.* Windsor: National Foundation for Educational Research.

Department of Education and Science. (1983). *Young People in the Eighties.* London: HMSO.

Dex, S. (1979). 'Job search methods and ethnic discrimination'. *New Community* 7, 1, pp. 31–39.

Dondy, F. (1974). 'The black explosion in schools'. *Race Today* 6, 2, pp. 44–47.

Ehrlich, H. (1973). *The Social Psychology of Prejudice.* New York: Wiley.

Erikson, E. H. (1966). 'The concept of identity in race relations: notes and queries'. *Daedalus* 95, pp. 145–171.

Evans, P. (1972). *Attitudes of Young Immigrants.* London: Runnymede Trust.

Fanon, F. (1968). *Black Skin: White Masks.* London: MacGibbon and Kee.

Field, S., Mair, G., Rees, T. and Stevens, P. (1981). *Ethnic Minorities in Britain: a study of trends in their position since 1961.* Home Office Research Study No. 68. London: HMSO.

Fisher, G. and Joshua, H. (1982). 'Social policy and black youth'. In Cashmore, E. and Troyna, B. (Eds.) *Black Youth in Crisis.* London: Allen and Unwin.

Foner, N. (1977) 'The Jamaicans'. In Watson, J. L. (Ed.) *Between Two Cultures: migrants and minorities in Britain.* Oxford: Blackwell.

Fowler, B. Littlewood, B. and Madigan, R. (1977). 'Immigrant school leavers and the search for work'. *Sociology* 11, 1, pp. 65–85.

Gaskell, G. and Smith, P. (1981a). *Race and "Alienated Youth" A Conceptual and Empirical Enquiry.* London: London School of Economics.

Gaskell, G. and Smith, P. (1981b). ''Alienated' black youth: an investigation of 'conventional wisdom' explanations'. *New Community,* 9, 2, pp. 182–193.

Gaskell, G. and Smith, P. (1982). 'The attitudes and aspirations of deprived black youth'. *Home Office Research Bulletin* 13, pp. 7–9.

Gregor, A. J. and Mcpherson, D. A. (1966). 'Racial preference and ego-identity among white and Bantu children in the Republic of South Africa'. *Genetic Psychology Monograph* 73, pp. 217–254.

Gupta, Y. P. (1977). 'The educational and vocational aspirations of Asian immigrant and English school-leavers: a comparative study'. *British Journal of Sociology* 28, 2, pp. 185–198.

Hill, D. (1970). 'The attitudes of West Indian and English adolescents in Britain'. *Race*, 11, 3, pp. 313–321.

Home Office (1981). *Racial Attacks: Report of a Home Office Study.* London: Home Office.

Hough, M. and Mayhew, P. (1983). *The British Crime Survey: a first report.* Home Office Research Study No. 76. London: HMSO.

Hraba, J. and Grant, G. (1970). 'Black is beautiful: a re-examination of racial preference and identification'. *Journal of Personality and Social Psychology* 16, 3, pp. 398–402.

Jelinek, M. M. (1977). 'Multiracial education 3. Pupils attitudes to the multiracial school'. *Educational Research* 19, 2, pp. 129–141.

Jelinek, M. M. and Brittan, E. M. (1975). 'Multiracial education 1. Inter-ethnic friendship patterns'. *Educational Research* 18, 1, pp. 44–53.

John, G. (1972). *Race in the Inner City.* London: Runnymede Trust.

Kawwa, T. (1968). 'Three sociometric studies of ethnic relations in London schools'. *Race* 10, 2, pp. 177–180.

Lawrence, E. (1982). 'In the abundance of water the fool is thirsty: sociology and black "pathology" '. In Centre for Contemporary Cultural Studies. *The Empire Strikes Back: race and racism in 70s Britain.* London: Hutchinson.

Lee, G. and Wrench, J. (1983). *Skill seekers: black youths, apprenticeships and disadvantage.* Leicester: National Youth Bureau.

Levine and Nayar, T. (1975). 'Modes of adaptation by Asian immigrants in Slough' *New Community* 4, 3, pp. 356–365.

Lomax, P. (1977). 'The self-concepts of girls in the context of a disadvantaging environment'. *Educational Review* 29, pp. 107–119.

Louden, D. (1977). *A Comparative Study of Self-esteem and Locus of Control in Minority Group Adolescents.* Ph.D. thesis. University of Bristol.

Louden, D. (1981). 'A comparative study of self-concepts among minority and majority group adolescents in English multiracial schools'. *Ethnic and Racial Studies,* 4, 2, pp. 153–174.

Madge, N. J. H. (1976). 'Context and the expressed preferences of infant school children'. *Journal of Child Psychology and Psychiatry* 17, 4, pp. 377–344.

McCaghy, C. H. (1968). 'Public attitudes toward city police in a middle sized northern city'. *Criminologica,* 6.

Mil Research Ltd. (1979). *Attitudes to the Police.* Unpublished report prepared for the Central Office of Information.

Miles, R. (1978). *Between two cultures? The case of Rastafarianism.* Working paper on ethnic relations no. 10. Bristol: SSRC Research Unit on Ethnic Relations.

Milner, D. (1975). *Children and Race.* Harmondsworth: Penguin.

Morland, J. (1969). 'Race awareness among American and Hong Kong Chinese children'. *American Journal of Sociology* 75, pp. 360–374.

Moynihan, D. P. (1965). *The Negro Family: the case for national action.* Washington DC: United States Department of Labor.

Nandy, D. (1969). 'Unrealistic aspirations'. *Race Today* 1, 1, pp. 9–11.

Nowikowski, S, and Ward, R. (1979). 'Middle class and British? — An analysis of south Asians in suburbia'. *New Community* 7, 1, pp. 1–10.

Office of Population Censuses and Surveys. (1980). *Young Peoples Employment Study:* Preliminary Report no. 4.

Phizacklea, A-M. (1975). 'A sense of political efficacy: a comparison of black and white adolescents'. In Crewe, I. (Ed.) *The Politics of Race.* London: Croom Helm.

Pirani, M. (1974). 'Aspirations and expectations of English and immigrant youth'. *New Community* 3, 1–2.

Pollak, M. (1979). *Nine Years Old.* Lancaster: MTP Press.

Proshansky, H. and Newton, P. (1973). 'Colour: the nature and meaning of negro self-identity'. In Watson, P. (Ed.) *Psychology and Race.* Harmondsworth: Penguin Education.

Pryce, K. (1978). 'Lifestyles of West Indians in Britain: a study of Bristol'. *New Community* 6, 3, pp. 207–217.

Pryce, K. (1979). *Endless Pressure.* Harmondsworth: Penguin.

Pushkin, I. and Veness, T. 'The development of racial awareness and prejudice in children'. In Watson, P. (Ed.) *Psychology and Race.* Harmondsworth: Penguin Education.

Ratcliffe, P. (1981). *Racism and Reaction.* London: Routledge.

Rex, J. (1982). 'West Indian and Asian youth'. In Cashmore, E. and Troyna, B. (Eds.) *Black Youth in Crisis.* London: Allen and Unwin.

Richardson, S. A. and Green, A. (1971). 'When is black beautiful? Coloured and white children's reactions to skin colour'. *British Journal of Educational Psychology* 41, pp. 62–69.

Roberts, K. Duggan, J. and Noble, M. (1981). 'Ignoring the sign: young, unemployed and unregistered'. *Department of Employment Gazette,* 89, 8, pp. 353–356.

Robertson, T. S. and Kawwa, T. (1971). 'Ethnic relations in a girls comprehensive school'. *Educational Research* 13, 3, pp. 214–217.

Rowley, K. G. (1968). 'Social relations between British and immigrant children'. *Educational Research* 10, 2, pp. 145–148.

Saeed, S. and Galbraith, J. I. (1982). 'Attitudes of Asian children to the police'. *New Community* 9, 3, pp. 447–453.

Sartre, J. P. (1960). *Anti-semite and Jew.* New York: Grove Press.

Select Committee on Race Relations and Immigration. (1969). *The Problems of Coloured School-leavers.* vol. II. London: HMSO.

Sharma, S. M. (1980). 'Perception of political institutions among Asian and English adolescents in Britain'. *New Community* 7, 3, pp. 240–247.

Small, S. (1983). *Police and People in London II: a group of young black people.* London: PSI.

Smith, D. J. (1976). *The Facts of Racial Disadvantage.* London: PEP.

Smith, D. J. (1981). *Unemployment and Racial Minorities.* London: PSI.

Smith, D. J. (1983). *Police and People in London I: a survey of Londoners.* London: PSI.

Southgate, P. (1982). 'The disturbances of July 1981 in Handsworth, Birmingham'. In Field, S. and Southgate, P. *Public Disorder.* Home Office Research Study No. 72. London: HMSO.

Stevens, P. and Willis, C. (1981). *Ethnic Minorities and Complaints Against the Police.* Research and Planning Unit Paper no. 5. London: Home Office.

Stevenson, D. and Wallis, P. (1970). 'Second generation West Indians: a study in alienation'. *Race Today* 2, 8, pp. 278–280.

Tajfel, H. (1981). *Human Groups and Social Categories.* Cambridge: Cambridge University Press.

Taylor, M. (1981). *Caught Between: a review of research into the education of pupils of West Indian origin.* Windsor: NFER and Nelson.

Troyna, B. (1979). 'Differential commitment to ethnic identity by black youths in Britain'. *New Community* 7, 3, pp. 406–421.

Tuck, M. and Southgate, P. (1981). *Ethnic Minorities, Crime and Policing.* Home Office Research Study No. 70. London: HMSO.

Vaughan, G. M. (1964a). 'Ethnic awareness in relation to minority group membership'. *Journal of Genetic Psychology* 105, pp. 119–130.

Vaughan, G. M. (1964b). 'The development of ethnic attitudes in New Zealand school-children'. *Genetic Psychology Monograph* 70, pp. 135–175.

Verma, G. K. (1975). 'Inter-group prejudice and race relations'. In Verma, G. K. and Bagley, C. *Race and Education Across Cultures.* London: Heinemann.

Ward, S. H. and Braun, J. (1972). 'Self-esteem and racial preference in black children'. *American Journal of Orthopsychiatry* 42, 4, pp. 644–647.

Watson, J. L. (Ed.) (1977). *Between Two Cultures.* Oxford: Blackwell.

Whitehouse, R. (1973). 'The cultural background of West Indian children in relation to their education aspirations'. *Journal of Applied Educational Studies* 2, 1, pp. 10–18.

Wild, R. and Ridgway, C. C. (1970). 'The job expectations of immigrant workers'. *Race* 11, 3, pp. 323–333.

Ziller, R. (1972). *The Social Self.* Elmsford: Pergamon.

Publications

Titles already published for the Home Office

Postage extra

Studies in the Causes of Delinquency and the Treatment of Offenders (SCDTO)

1. Prediction methods in relation to borstal training. Hermann Mannheim and Leslie T. Wilkins. 1955. viii + 276pp. (11 340051 9).

2. *Time spent awaiting trial. Evelyn Gibson. 1960. v + 45pp. (34–368–2).

3. *Delinquent generations. Leslie T. Wilkins. 1960. iv + 20pp. (11 340053 5).

4. *Murder. Evelyn Gibson and S. Klein. 1961. iv + 44pp. (11 340054 3).

5. Persistent criminals. A study of all offenders liable to preventive detention in 1956. W. H. Hammond and Edna Chayen. 1963. ix + 237pp. (34–368–5).

6. *Some statistical and other numerical techniques for classifying individuals. P. McNaughton-Smith. 1965. v + 33pp. (34–368–6).

7. Probation research: a preliminary report. Part I. General outline of research. Part II. Study of Middlesex probation area (SOMPA). Steven Folkard, Kate Lyon, Margaret M. Carver and Erica O'Leary. 1966. vi + 58pp. (11 340374 7).

8. *Probation research: national study of probation. Trends and regional comparisons in probation (England and Wales). Hugh Barr and Erica O'Leary. 1966. vii + 51pp. (34–368–8).

9. *Probation research. A survey of group work in the probation service. Hugh Barr. 1966. vii + 94pp. (34–368–9).

10. *Types of delinquency and home background. A validation study of Hewitt and Jenkins' hypothesis. Elizabeth Field. 1967. vi + 21pp. (34–368–10).

11. *Studies of female offenders. No. 1—Girls of 16–20 years sentencd to borstal or detention centre training in 1963. No. 2—Women offenders in the Metropolitan Police District in March and April 1957. No. 3—A description of women in prison on January 1, 1965. Nancy Goodman and Jean Price. 1967 v + 78pp. (34–368–11).

12. *The use of the Jesness Inventory on a sample of British probationers. Martin Davies. 1967. iv + 20pp. (34–368–12).

13. *The Jesness Inventory: application to approved school boys. Joy Mott. 1969. iv + 27pp. (11 340063 2).

Home Office Research Studies (HORS)

1. *Workloads in children's departments. Eleanor Grey. 1969. vi + 75pp. (11 340101 9).

2. *Probationers in their social environment. A study of male probationers aged 17–20, together with an analysis of those reconvicted within twelve months. Martin Davies. 1969. vii + 204pp. (11 340102 7).

3. *Murder 1957 to 1968. A Home Office Statistical Division report on murder in England and Wales. Evelyn Gibson and S. Klein (with annex by the Scottish Home and Health Department on murder in Scotland). 1969. vi + 94pp. (11 340103 5).

4. Firearms in crime. A Home Office Statistical Division report on indicatable offences involving firearms in England and Wales. A. D. Weatherhead and B. M. Robinson. 1970. viii + 39pp. (11 340104 3).

---

*Out of print. Photostat copies can be purchased from HMSO upon request.

5. *Financial penalties and probation. Martin Davies. 1970. vii + 39pp. (11 340105 1).

6. *Hostels for probationers. A study of the aims, working and variations in effectiveness of male probation hostels with special reference to the influence of the environment on delinquency. Ian Sinclair. 1971. ix + 200pp. (11 340106 X).

7. *Prediction methods in criminology — including a prediction study of young men on probation. Frances H. Simon. 1971. xi + 234pp. (11 340107 8).

8. *Study of the juvenile liaison scheme in West Ham 1961–65. Marilyn Taylor. 1971. vi + 46pp. (11 340108 6).

9. *Explorations in after-care. I — After-care units in London, Liverpool and Manchester. Martin Silberman (Royal London Prisoners' Aid Society) and Brenda Chapman. II — After-care hostels receiving a Home Office grant. Ian Sinclair and David Snow (HORU). III — St. Martin of Tours House, Aryeh Leissner (National Bureau for Co-operation in Child Care). 1971. xi + !40pp. (11 340109 4).

10. *A survey of adoption in Great Britain. Eleanor Grey in collaboration with Ronald M. Blunden. 1971. ix + 168pp. (11 340110 8).

11. *Thirteen-year-old approved school boys in 1962s. Elizabeth Field, W. H. Hammond and J. Tizard. 1971. ix + 46pp. (11 340111 6).

12. Absconding from approved schools. R. V. G. Clarke and D. N. Martin. 1971. vi + 146pp. (11 340112 4).

13. An experiment in personality assessment of young men remanded in custody. H. Sylvia Anthony. 1972. viii + 79pp. (11 340113 2).

14. *Girl offenders aged 17–20 years. I — Statistics relating to girl offenders aged 17–20 years from 1960 to 1970. II — Re-offending by girls released from borstal or detention centre training. III — The problems of girls released from borstal training during their period on after-care. Jean Davies and Nancy Goodman. 1972. v + 77p. (11 340114 0).

15. *The controlled trial in institutional research — paradigm or pitfall for penal evaluators? R. V. G. Clarke and D. B. Cornish. 1972. v + 33pp. (11 340115 9).

16. *A survey of fine enforcement. Paul Softley. 1973. v + 65pp. (11 340116 7).

17. *An index of social environment — designed for use in social work research. Martin Davies. 1973. vi + 63pp. (11 340117 5).

18. *Social enquiry reports and the probation service. Martin Davies and Andrea Knopf. 1973. v + 49pp. (11 340118 3).

19. *Depression, psychopathic personality and attempted suicide in a borstal sample. H. Sylvia Anthony. 1973. viii + 44pp. (0 11 340119 1).

20. *The use of bail and custody by London magistrates' courts before and after the Criminal Justice Act 1967. Frances Simon and Mollie Weatheritt. 1974. vi + 78pp. (0 11 340120 5).

21. *Social work in the environment. A study of one aspect of probation practice. Martin Davies, with Margaret Rayfield, Alaster Calder and Tony Fowles. 1974. ix + 151pp. (0 11 340121 3).

22 Social work in prison. An experiment in the use of extended contact with offenders. Margaret Shaw. 1974. viii + 154pp. (0 11 340122 1).

23. Delinquency amongst opiate users. Joy Mott and Marilyn Taylor. 1974. vi + 31pp. (0 11 340663 0).

24. IMPACT. Intensive matched probation and after-care treatment. Vol. I — The design of the probation experiment and an interim evaluation. M. S. Folkard, A. J. Fowles, B. C. McWilliams, W. McWilliams, D. D. Smith, D. E. Smith and G. R. Walmsley. 1974. v + 54pp. (0 11 340664 9).

25. The approved school experience. An account of boys' experiences of training under differing regimes of approved schools, with an attempt to evaluate the effectiveness of that training. Anne B. Dunlop. 1974. vii + 124pp. (0 11 340665 7).

26. *Absconding from open prisons. Charlotte Banks, Patricia Mayhew and R. J. Sapsford. 1975. viii + 89pp. (0 11 340666 5).

27. Driving while disqualified. Sue Kriefman. 1975. vi + 136pp. (0 11 340667 3).

---

*Out of print. Photostat copies can be purchased from HMSO upon request.

28. Some male offenders' problems. I — Homeless offenders in Liverpool. W. McWilliams. II — Casework with short-term prisoners. Julie Holborn. 1975. x + 147pp. (0 11 340668 1).

29. *Community service orders. K. Pease, P. Durkin, I. Earnshaw, D. Payne and J. Thorpe. 1975. viii + 80pp. (0 11 340669 X).

30. Field Wing Bail Hostel: the first nine months. Frances Simon and Sheena Wilson. 1975. viii + 55pp. (0 11 340670 3).

31. Homicide in England and Wales 1967–1971. Evelyn Gibson. 1975. iv + 59pp. (0 11 340753 X).

32. Residential treatment and its effects on delinquency. D. B. Cornish and R. V. G. Clarke. 1975. vi + 74pp. (0 11 340672 X).

33. Further studies of female offenders. Part A: Borstal girls eight years after release. Nancy Goodman, Elizabeth Maloney and Jean Davies. Part B: The sentencing of women at the London Higher Courts. Nancy Goodman, Paul Durkin and Janet Halton. Part C: Girls appearing before a juvenile court. Jean Davies. 1976. vi + 114pp. (0 11 340673 8).

34. *Crime as opportunity. P. Mayhew, R. V. G. Clarke, A. Sturman and J. M. Hough. 1976. vii + 36pp. (0 11 340674 6).

35. The effectiveness of sentencing: a review of the literature. S. R. Brody. 1976. v + 89pp. (0 11 340675 4).

36. IMPACT. Intensive matched probation and after-care treatment. Vol II — The results of the experiment. M. S. Folkard, D. E. Smith and D. D. 1976. xi + 400pp. (0 11 340676 2).

37. Police cautioning in England and Wales. J. A. Ditchfield. 1976. v + 31pp. (0 11 340677 0).

38. Parole in England and Wales. C. P. Nuttall, with E. E. Barnard, A. J. Fowles, A. Frost, W. H. Hammond, P. Mayhew, K. Pease, R. Tarling and M. J. Weatheritt. 1977. vi + 90pp. (0 11 340678 9).

39. Community service assessed in 1976. K. Pease, S. Billingham and I. Earnshaw. 1977. vi + 29pp. (0 11 340679 7).

40. Screen violence and film censorship: a review of research. Stephen Brody. 1977. vii + 179pp. (0 11 340680 0).

41. Absconding from borstals. Gloria K. Laycock. 1977. v + 82pp. (0 11 340681 9).

42. Gambling: a review of the literature and its implications for policy and research. D. B. Cornish. 1978. xii + 284pp. (0 11 340682 7).

43. Compensation orders in magistrates' courts. Paul Softley. 1978. v + 41pp. (0 11 340683 5).

44. Research in criminal justice. John Croft. 1978. iv + 16pp. (0 11 340684 3).

45. Prison welfare: an account of an experiment at Liverpool. A. J. Fowles. 1978. v + 34pp. (0 11 340685 1).

46. Fines in magistrates' courts. Paul Softley. 1978. v + 42pp. (0 11 340686 X).

47. Tackling vandalism. R. V. G. Clarke (editor), F. J. Gladstone, A. Sturman and Sheena Wilson (contributors). 1978. vi + 91pp. (0 11 340687 8).

48. Social inquiry reports: a survey. Jennifer Thorpe. 1979. vi + 55pp. (0 11 340688 6).

49. Crime in public view. P. Mayhew, R. V. G. Clarke, J. N. Burrows, J. M. Hough and S. W. C. Winchester. 1979. v + 36pp. (0 11 340689 4).

50. Crime and the community. John Croft. 1979. v + 16pp. (0 11 340690 8).

51. Life-sentence prisoners. David Smith (editor), Christopher Brown, Joan Worth, Roger Sapsford and Charlotte Banks (contributors). 1979. iv + 51pp. (0 11 340691 6).

52. Hostels for offenders. Jane E. Andrews, with an appendix by Bill Sheppard. 1979. v + 30pp. (0 11 340692 4).

53. Previous convictions, sentence and reconviction: a statistical study of a sample of 5,000 offenders convicted in January 1971. G. J. O. Phillpotts and L. B. Lancucki, 1979. v + 55pp. (0 11 340693 2).

54. Sexual offences, consent and sentencing. Roy Walmsley and Karen White. 1979. vi + 77pp. (0 11 340694 0).

---

*Out of print. Photostat copies can be purchased from HMSO upon request.

55. Crime prevention and the police. John Burrows, Paul Ekblom and Kevin Heal. 1979. v + 37pp. (0 11 340695 9).

56. Sentencing practice in magistrates' courts. Roger Tarling, with the assistance of Mollie Weatheritt. 1979. vii + 54pp. (0 11 340696 7).

57. Crime and comparative research. John Croft. 1979. iv + 16pp. (0 11 340697 5).

58. Race, crime and arrests. Philip Stevens and Carole F. Willis. 1979. v + 69pp. (0 11 340698 3).

59. Research and criminal policy. John Croft. 1980. iv + 14pp. (0 11 340699 1).

60. Junior attendance centres. Anne B. Dunlop. 1980. v + 47pp. (0 11 340700 9).

61. Police interrogation: an observational study in four police stations. Paul Softley, with the assistance of David Brown, Bob Forde, George Mair and David Moxon. 1980. vii + 67pp. (0 11 340701 7).

62. Co-ordinating crime prevention efforts. F. J. Gladstone. 1980. v + 74pp. (0 11 340702 5).

63. Crime prevention publicity: an assessment. D. Riley and P. Mayhew. 1980. v + 47pp. (0 11 340703 3).

64. Taking offenders out of circulation. Stephen Brody and Roger Tarling. 1980. v + 46pp. (0 11 340704 1).

65. *Alcoholism and social policy: are we on the right lines? Mary Tuck. 1980. v + 30pp. (0 11 340705 X).

66. Persistent petty offenders. Suzan Fairhead. 1981. vi + 78pp. (0 11 340706 8).

67. Crime control and the police. Pauline Morris and Kevin Heal. 1981. v + 71pp. (0 11 340707 6).

68. Ethnic minorities in Britain: a study of trends in their position since 1961. Simon Field, George Mair, Tom Rees and Philip Stevens. 1981. v + 48pp. (0 11 340708 4).

69. Managing criminological research. John Croft. 1981. iv + 17pp. (0 11 340709 2).

70. Ethnic minorities, crime and policing: a survey of the experiences of West Indians and whites. Mary Tuck and Peter Southgate. 1981. iv + 54pp. (0 11 340765 3).

71. Contested trials in magistrates' courts. Julie Vennard. 1982. v + 32pp. (0 11 340766 1).

72. Public disorder: a review of research and a study in one inner city area. Simon Field and Peter Southgate. 1982. v + 77pp. (0 11 340767 X).

73. Clearing up crime. John Burrows and Roger Tarling. 1982. vii + 31pp. (0 11 340768 8).

74. Residential burglary: the limits of prevention. Stuart Winchester and Hilary Jackson. 1982. v + 47pp. (0 11 340769 6).

75. Concerning crime. John Croft. 1982. iv + 16pp. (0 11 340770 X).

76. The British Crime Survey: first report. Mike Hough and Pat Mayhew. 1983. v + 62pp. (0 11 340786 6).

77. Contacts between police and public: findings from the British Crime Survey. Peter Southgate and Paul Ekblom. 1984. v + 42pp. (0 11 340771 8).

78. Fear of crime in England and Wales. Michael Maxfield. 1984. v + 51pp. (0 11 340772 6).

79. Crime and police effectiveness. Ronald V. Clarke and Mike Hough. 1984. iv + 33pp. (0 11 340773 4).

ALSO

Designing out crime. R. V. G. Clarke and P. Mayhew (editors). 1980. viii + 186pp. (0 11 340732 7).
(This book collects, with an introduction, studies that were originally published in HORS 34, 47, 49, 55, 62 and 63 and which are illustrative of the 'situational' approach to crime prevention.)

The above HMSO publications can be purchased from Government Bookshops or through booksellers.

*Out of print. Photostat copies can be purchased from HMSO upon request.

The following Home Office research publications are available on request from the Home Office Research and Planning Unit, 50 Queen Anne's Gate, London, SW1H 9AT.

Research Unit Papers (RUP)

1. Uniformed police work and management technology. J. M. Hough. 1980.

2. Supplementary information on sexual offences and sentencing. Roy Walmsley and Karen White. 1980.

3. Board of visitor adjudications. David Smith, Claire Austin and John Ditchfield. 1981.

4. Day centres and probations. Suzan Fairhead, with the assistance of J. Wilkinson-Grey. 1981.

Research and Planning unit Papers (RPUP)

5. Ethnic minorities and complaints against the police. Philip Stevens and Carole Willis. 1982.

6. Crime and public housing. Mike Hough and Pat Mayhew (editors). 1982.

7. Abstracts of race relations research. George Mair and Philip Stevens (editors). 1982.

8. Police probationer training in race relations. Peter Southgate. 1982.

9. The police response to calls from the public. Paul Ekblom and Kevin Heal. 1982.

10. City centre crime: a situational approach to prevention. Malcolm Ramsay. 1982.

11. Burglary in schools: the prospects for prevention. Tim Hope. 1982.

12. Fine enforcement. Paul Softley and David Moxon. 1982.

13. Vietnamese refugees. Peter Jones. 1982.

14. Community resources for victims of crime. Karen Williams. 1983.

15. The use, effectiveness and impact of police stop and search powers. Carole Willis. 1983.

16. Acquittal rates. Sid Butler. 1983.

17. Criminal justice comparisons: the case of Scotland and England and Wales. Lorna J. F. Smith. 1983.

18. Time taken to deal with juveniles under criminal proceedings. Catherine Frankenburg and Roger Tarling. 1983.

19. Civilian review of complaints against the police: a survey of the United States literature. David C. Brown. 1983.

20. Police action on motoring offences. David Riley. 1983.

21. Diverting drunks from the criminal justice system. Sue Kingsley and George Mair. 1983.

22. The staff resource implications of an independent prosecution system. Peter R. Jones. 1983.

23. Reducing the prison population: an explanatory study in Hampshire. David Smith, Bill Sheppard, George Mair and Karen Williams. 1984.

24. Criminal justice system model: magistrates' courts' sub-model. Susan Rice. 1984.

Research Bulletin

The Research Bulletin is published twice a year and consists mainly of short articles relating to projects which are part of the Home Office Research and Planning Unit's research programme.

Printed in the UK for HMSO
Dd 737740 C25 5/84